GRADES 4–6

Make writing fun for your students with *The Best Of The Mailbox® Writing!* This compilation of ideas and activities—selected from 1990–1998 issues of *The Mailbox®* magazine for intermediate teachers—will energize your writing lessons while strengthening students' writing skills. Inside this invaluable classroom resource, you'll find:

- Thematic Writing Units
- Skill-Based Reproducibles
- Patterns
- Journal Prompts
- Motivational Writing Ideas and Tips
- Management and Organizational Ideas
- Bulletin Boards

Editor
Elizabeth H. Lindsay

Art Coordinator
Barry Slate

Cover Artist
Nick Greenwood

www.themailbox.com

©1999 by THE EDUCATION CENTER, INC.
All rights reserved.
ISBN #1-56234-339-4

Except as provided for herein, no part of this publication may be reproduced or transmitted in any form or by any means, electronic or mechanical, including photocopying, recording, or storing in any information storage and retrieval system or electronic online bulletin board, without prior written permission from The Education Center, Inc. Permission is given to the original purchaser to reproduce patterns and reproducibles for individual classroom use only and not for resale or distribution. Reproduction for an entire school or school system is prohibited. Please direct written inquiries to The Education Center, Inc., P.O. Box 9753, Greensboro, NC 27429-0753. The Education Center®, *The Mailbox®*, and the mailbox/post/grass logo are registered trademarks of The Education Center, Inc.. All other brand or product names are trademarks or registered trademarks of their respective companies.

Manufactured in the United States
10 9 8 7 6 5 4 3

Table of Contents

Writing Units 4–46
  Step Right Up to Writing Essays 4–10
  A Dynamic Duo! 11–15
  A Dynamic Duo: Part 2 16–20
  Writing Workshop Wisdom 21–25
  You Oughta Be in Print 26–30
  Paragraph Pointers 31–42
  Cool Writing for Cold Days 43–46

Journal Topics 48–76
  Tips For Using Journals and Topics 48
  August Journal Topics 49–50
  September Journal Topics 51–52
  October Journal Topics 53–54
  November Journal Topics 55–56
  December Journal Topics 57–58
  January Journal Topics 59–60
  February Journal Topics 61–62
  March Journal Topics 63–64
  April Journal Topics 65–66
  May Journal Topics 67–68
  June Journal Topics 69
  July Journal Topics 70
  August/September Journal Covers 71
  October/November Journal Covers 72
  December/January Journal Covers 73
  February/March Journal Covers 74
  April/May Journal Covers 75
  June/July Journal Covers 76

Write On! 78–94

Our Readers Write 96–102

Bulletin Boards 104–110

Answer Key 112

Step Right Up To Writing Essays

Take a giant step toward better student essays with the following "shoe-fire" activities and reproducibles—all guaranteed to bring students to their feet!

with ideas by Terry Healy

A Footnote On Essays

An *essay* is a short composition that has one main idea. It may require some research and often contains the writer's personal opinions. A person writing an essay should pick a topic that interests her, she already knows something about, and she has a strong opinion about. There are three basic types of essays:

- *Informational essay:* presents important facts about a subject or teaches a new skill. It's like a report, but is shorter and not as detailed.
- *Persuasive essay:* presents the author's opinion, backed up by believable supporting details. The author tries to convince a reader to agree with his point of view.
- *Personal essay:* shares the writer's thoughts about a fun or serious subject related to his personal life. The goal is to entertain readers or express feelings about a subject.

Using This Unit

The first six activities in this unit are on basic essay-writing skills that pertain to writing any type of essay. You'll also find a list of terrific Internet connections to use when teaching about essay writing. The unit concludes with creative ideas that provide practice on writing each of the three different types of essays.

Essay-Writing Skills

A "Shoe" Fit

Skill: Choosing a topic

Help students learn how to choose an essay topic that's a "shoe" fit with this activity. In advance write each of these topics on two slips of paper: Sports, Friends, Buildings, Food, Clothes, Music, Animals, School, Books, Careers, Family, Movies, Transportation, Computers, Television. Place the slips in a shoebox. After reviewing the three types of essays (see above), explain to students that sometimes a writer chooses a topic that's too broad or too narrow. Write "Holidays" on the board. Ask if this topic is too broad, too narrow, or a good fit for an essay *(too broad)*. Then write "Christmas Sugar Cookies" on the board and repeat the question *(too narrow)*. Finally web the broad topic "Holidays" with the class. Based on the web, help students identify topics that would be good fits for an essay.

Next have each child draw a slip from the shoebox and web its topic on her paper. After the web is complete, have the student remove one shoe and trace her socked foot on colorful paper. Then have her cut out the tracing and label it with three to five good essay topics from her web. Collect these cutouts; then place a small sticker beside each topic that is a good fit for an essay. Post the cutouts on a large piece of bulletin-board paper titled "Topics That Are A 'Shoe' Fit!" Have students refer to this poster whenever they need an essay topic.

Don't Forget The Details!
Skill: Developing details

An essay without details is like a television show without color—pretty dull! To help students get the hang of coloring their essays with details, write the following questions on the board: "Who? What? Where? When? How?" Also list the five senses—*touch, taste, hearing, sight,* and *smell*—and the following topics:
- The day you first met your best friend
- Your first day in this class
- When you finally overcame a big fear
- The day you got your pet
- The last time you ate ice cream
- The time you won a hard-fought game

Ask each student to select one of the topics; then have him list details from that experience to answer the five questions on the board. Encourage students to also include sensory details in their answers.

Next give each student a white paper plate. Have the student write his topic in the center of the plate with a marker. Then have him surround his topic with at least five descriptive sentences about it—each written with a different color of fine-tipped marker. After students share their sentences, post the plates on a bulletin board titled "Color Your Essay With Details!"

A Step Above The Rest
Skill: Planning an essay

Writing an essay that's a step above the rest is a cinch when you've got a good plan! The reproducible on page 9 features a step-by-step outline for planning an essay. Give each student a copy of the page. Go over the outline with your class. Then assign the first essay (for ideas on specific essays to write, see pages 7–8). Duplicate extra copies of the reproducible to have on hand for planning essays throughout your unit.

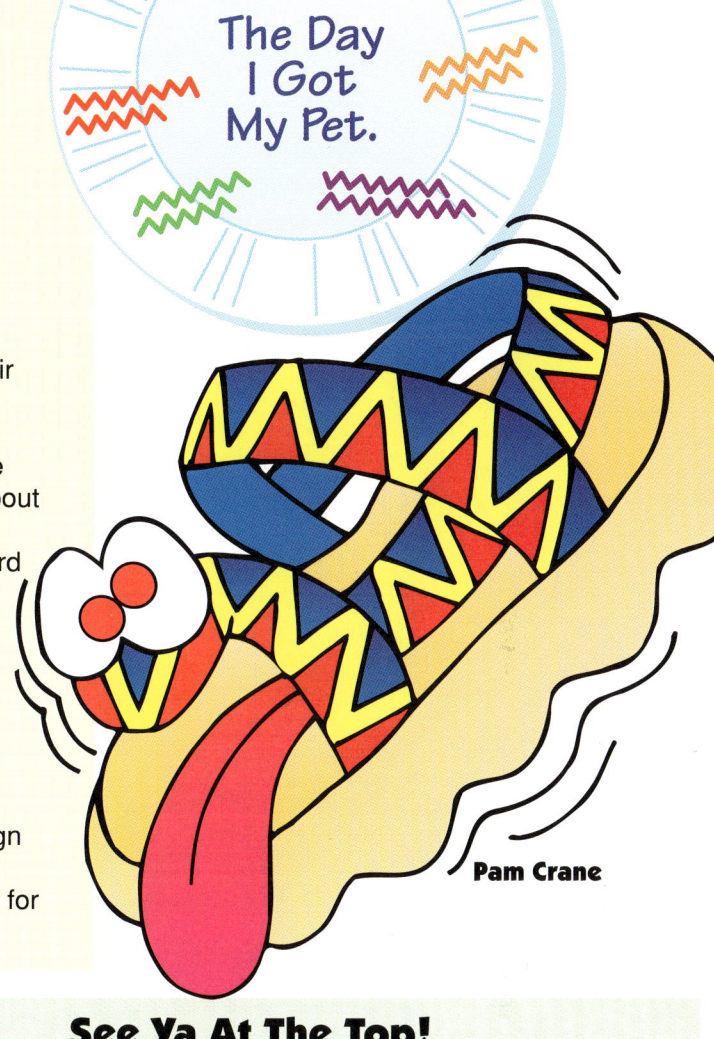

Pam Crane

See Ya At The Top!
Skill: Writing an introductory paragraph

A good writer knows to top off a great essay with an attention-grabbing introduction! Help students learn how to write good introductory paragraphs with this group activity. Collect four or five brief essays or letters to the editors from several popular children's magazines. (Ask your media specialist for help.) Clip a large index card onto each essay to conceal its introductory paragraph; then give one essay to each student group.

Next review with students these guidelines for writing a good introductory paragraph:
- Include a few sentences that tell your point of view, give a reason for the reader to read the essay, and tell the reader the purpose of the essay.
- Grab the reader's attention by opening with a question, a quotation, or a unique statement.

Distribute one essay to each group. Have the group read its essay together, then collaborate to write a four- or five-sentence introduction for it. After each group has finished, let students remove the index cards and compare their introductions to the original ones. Discuss students' reactions and insights as a class. If time allows, let groups put the index cards back on the original essays; then have them swap essays and repeat the exercise.

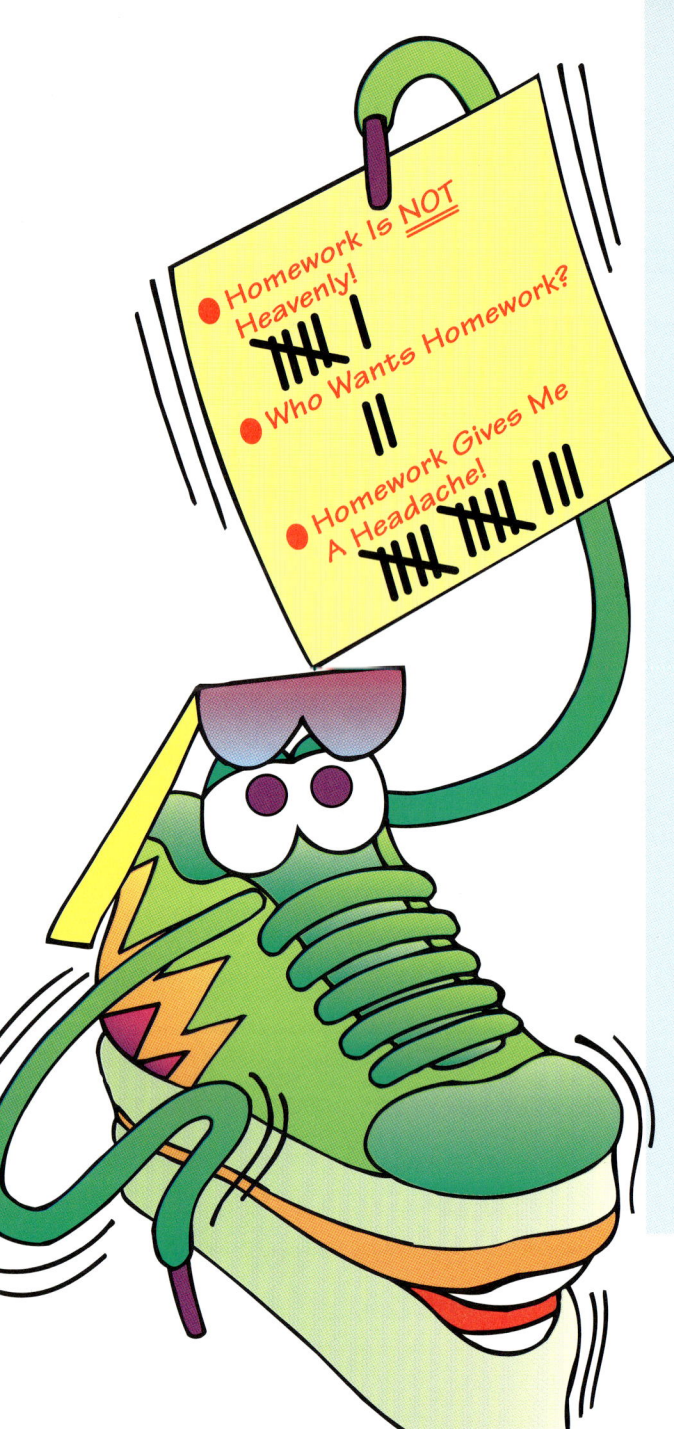

A Title Match
Skill: Choosing a title

Coming up with a good title for an essay is often difficult for students. Join forces to craft great essay titles with this fun activity. After you've assigned an essay and students have completed the reproducible essay planner on page 9 (see "A Step Above The Rest" on page 5), divide your class into groups. Instruct each group to review its members' planners and suggest titles for each essay. Remind students that a good title not only fits the essay but also grabs the reader's attention. Direct each student to write three of the titles suggested by his group on a Post-it® Brand note, leaving room beneath each title as shown. Then have him attach the note to his planner. Collect the planners and mount them on a bulletin board. Ask students to vote on their favorite title for each planner by drawing a tally mark beneath it on the note. After two days of voting, return each child's planner to him with its note. Then have students start working on their rough drafts.
Teamwork + titles = a perfect match for everyone's essay!

Making An Essay Shine!
Skill: Editing a rough draft

Once a rough draft has been written, it's time to polish it up. And the reproducible checklist on page 10 is just the tool for the job! First display a list of proofreading symbols you want students to use when editing their work. After each child has written her essay's rough draft, give her a copy of page 10. Have the student list the names of two other people who will edit her rough draft besides herself (you may wish to stipulate that you be one of the three editors). Then instruct her to complete the page as directed. After the third edit has been completed, have the essay and checklist returned to its original owner so she can begin revisions. After this great polish job, be ready for a finished essay that simply shines!

The Internet Connection

Take a look at these terrific Web sites that feature kids' writings, including examples of essays *(current as of 6/99)*:

- **http://www.kidpub.org:** KidPub, an outstanding publishing site, features student-written work (stories, essays, poems, etc.) that your kids can read, review, and critique. Plus you can hook up your class with key pals to discuss writing ideas and peer-edit each other's work.

- **http://www.cyberkids.com:** Enjoy *Cyberkids,* a quarterly on-line magazine by kids and for kids. Offering fiction, art, and news articles, this site also includes the "Launchpad" that lists other good children's sites.

Writing An Informational Essay

Storyboard Sequencing

Sequencing skills are often put to the test when writing an informational essay. Make sequencing a snap with the help of simple storyboards. Take a series of photographs that show a co-worker or student completing each of the following simple multistep tasks:
- wrapping a gift
- cutting out a paper snowflake
- sharpening a pencil
- tying a shoe
- drawing a stick person on a piece of paper

After the pictures are developed, mount each task's photos in sequence on a strip of poster board. Give a storyboard to each small group of students. Have each child (or each group working collaboratively) write a short informational essay to teach the skill displayed on his group's storyboard. Display the finished essays on a bulletin board with the storyboards. Or place the storyboards in a center for students to work with during free time. The next time a student must write an informational essay, suggest that he draw out a simple storyboard first—before he begins writing—to help organize his thoughts in the proper sequence.

Up Close And Personal

Provide practically painless practice in writing informational essays with this interviewing activity! Ask another teacher in your school (either one on your grade level or of a younger class) to have her class help with this project. Brainstorm with your students a list of interview questions that will help them get to know another child in your partner class. Encourage students to be creative in forming their questions since they will be using the information gathered to write interesting essays. Pare the list down to no more than ten questions, avoiding those that require only a yes/no answer. Provide each of your students with a duplicated copy of the questions.

Next pair each of your kids with a child in your partner class. Have your student interview his partner using the interview questions. After the interviews are over, direct each of your students to use his partner's answers to write an informational essay about his buddy. Bind the finished essays in a book to share with your partner class during a special Up Close And Personal party.

Writing A Persuasive Essay

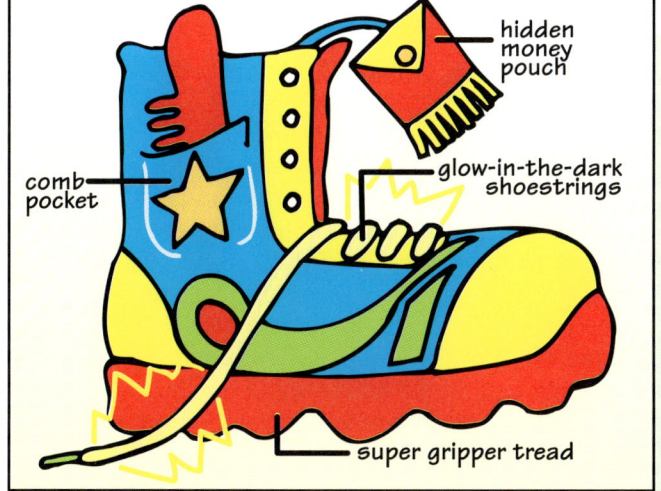

Steppin' Out In Style!

Watch out, Nike®! There will be a new group of shoe designers on the loose after this persuasive-essay activity! Divide your class into small groups. Give each group a large piece of art paper with instructions to design and color the ultimate new shoe for next year's market. After all designs are complete, have each team write a persuasive letter to the CEO of the Feet First Shoe Company. In this letter, have the group convince the executive that its shoe is sure to be the next best-seller. Remind each group to provide facts and details to support its assertion that its shoe is the best. Post the final drafts of the letters with their matching shoe designs on a bulletin board titled "Steppin' Out In Style!"

Time To Take Action!

Call students to action with this real-life writing assignment. Ask, "How would you make this school or community a better place?" Have students brainstorm while you list their ideas on the board; then select one problem as a class and develop a solution. Next display a transparency of the form shown. Explain to students that "Reason" means to list a reason or fact that will persuade someone to use your solution. Using transition words like *First* and *Also* helps the essay flow smoothly from one paragraph to another. Work together to fill out the form. Point out that students could now easily take the information on the form and write a persuasive essay about the problem. (You may want to complete this step with your class.)

For homework, provide each student with a blank copy of the form. Challenge each child to choose a different problem, fill out the form, and then use the form to write a persuasive essay. If appropriate, share completed essays with school or community officials.

Writing A Personal Essay

Oh, Bother!

For a personal-writing exercise that's no bother to do, try this kid-pleasin' idea! Brainstorm with students a list of pet peeves that *really* bother them. Then have each student choose one item and write a personal essay expressing his thoughts and feelings about the annoyance. Extend this activity on an upbeat note by having each student write another brief essay called "Learning To Live With My Pet Peeve."

For a math extension, list the topics of the students' essays on the board; then poll the class to find out who else is also annoyed by each pet peeve. Have students graph the class results.

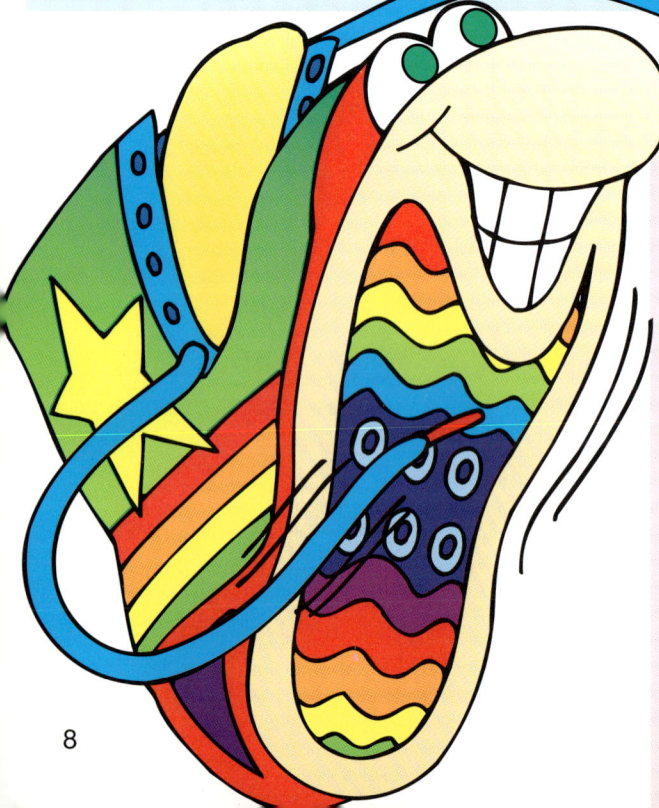

Walking In Your Shoes

Need a topic for a personal essay? Look no farther than your feet! With students, brainstorm a list of personal-essay topics related to shoes on the board. Some suggestions follow:
- My Most Favorite Shoes
- How Shoes Are Like People
- The Day I Got Cold Feet!
- Shoes I'd Like To Fill Someday
- My Time In The Footlights
- Thinking On My Feet

For homework ask each child to bring a shoe (or a picture of a shoe) to class. Also have the student describe in a brief paragraph a shoe-related topic on which he'd like to write a personal essay.

The next day have each student share his shoe and paragraph with the class. Provide time for you and the student's classmates to give feedback on his topic. Does it appear to be a comfortable fit for a personal essay, or does it need to be "resized"? After this sharing period, have each child write a personal essay about his topic. Display the essays and shoes on a table in your classroom or media center.

Name _____ Planning an essay

Steps To A Great Essay

A great essay begins with a great plan! Starting in the shoebox, use this sheet to plan an essay that's sure to be a step above all the rest. Use the back of this page if you need more space.

START HERE!

A. Select a topic: _____

B. Decide on the purpose of your essay (circle one): informational, persuasive, personal

C. Define your main idea: _____

① **Title:** should be descriptive and set the tone for the essay

_____

② **Introduction:**
- a few sentences that tell your point of view, give the reader a reason for reading the essay, and tell the reader the purpose of the essay
- opens with a question, a quotation, or an interesting statement

_____
_____

③ **Body:** explains or supports the main idea in several paragraphs. Each paragraph gives a main point about the topic with believable details.

Main point: _____

Details:
1. _____
2. _____
3. _____

Main point: _____

Details:
1. _____
2. _____
3. _____

Main point: _____

Details:
1. _____
2. _____
3. _____

④ **Conclusion:** repeats the main idea in a new way and wraps up the essay

Write notes for your conclusion on the back of this page.

©2000 The Education Center, Inc. • *The Best Of The Mailbox® Writing • Intermediate* • TEC1485

Note To The Teacher: Use with "A Step Above The Rest" on page 5.

Name _____ Editing a rough draft

Polishing Up A Rough Draft

You want your essay to really shine, right? Then start with polishing up your rough draft! First fill in the names of your second and third editors below. Then edit your draft according to the questions. After you edit for a question, check it off in the column labeled "1st edit." When you're finished, pass your essay and this checklist to the Second Editor. When your checklist and essay are returned, use the checklist and comments to help you write a final essay that really shines!

Second Editor: _____ Third Editor: _____

Questions	1st edit	2nd edit	3rd edit
1. Is the purpose of the essay clear and followed throughout the essay? Comments:			
2. Is the introduction interesting? Does it open with a question, a unique statement, or a quotation? Comments:			
3. Is the essay written in an organized and logical way? Comments:			
4. Are there at least three related main points to support the topic? Comments:			
5. Does the author include believable details to support the main points? Comments:			
6. Does the conclusion restate the main idea in a different way? Comments:			
7. Is the title descriptive, and does it do a good job of setting the tone of the essay? Comments:			
8. Does the author use the rules of good capitalization, punctuation, spelling, and grammar? Comments:			

©2000 The Education Center, Inc. • *The Best Of* The Mailbox *Writing* • Intermediate • TEC1485

Note To The Teacher: Use with "Making An Essay Shine!" on page 6.

Picture Books And Writing— A DYNAMIC DUO!
Using Picture Books To Teach Writing Skills

Looking for a way to make writing workshop a super success? Then pick up a picture book—"write" now! Use the following ideas from our readers to teach key writing skills through the pages of picture books.

Miss Yonkers Goes Bonkers
written by Mike Thaler and illustrated by Jared Lee
Avon Books

Skill: Descriptive writing

What kid wouldn't love a book about a teacher who wears a baseball cap and dances on her desk while humming "Girls Just Wanna Have Fun"? Use this hilarious tale about a teacher gone completely crazy to give students practice with descriptive writing. After reading the book to your class, challenge each student to write his own version titled "[your name] Goes Bonkers." Encourage students to include lots of details as they describe the day when *you* went a bit crazy at school. Bind the pages in a book that's sure to become a class favorite! *Jeffrey J. Kuntz—Grs. 4–6, West End Elementary, Punxsutawney, PA*

The Talking Eggs: A Folktale From The American South
retold by Robert D. San Souci
illustrated by Jerry Pinkney
E. P. Dutton, Inc.

Skill: Writing a fairy tale

When I want to introduce a unit on writing fairy tales, I pick up Robert D. San Souci's *The Talking Eggs*. It tells the story of two sisters—one kind, one selfish—and their very different encounters with an old woman and her magical talking eggs. After sharing the book with students, we discuss the elements of fairy tales. The next day I give each student a plastic Easter egg in which I've placed a small object, such as a penny, a pebble, or a bean. Each student then writes a brief fairy tale that incorporates his egg's item as a magical element in the story. It's a writing activity that's all it's cracked up to be! *Anita Perez—Gr. 5, Clyde Intermediate School, Clyde, TX*

Using Wordless Picture Books

Skill: Descriptive writing

Turn to wordless books the next time you want to sharpen descriptive-writing skills. Divide students into groups; then give each group a wordless picture book (ask your media specialist for good examples). Have each student in the group list verbs, adjectives, and adverbs that could be used to describe the story. Then have students in the group go over one another's lists, crossing out any repeated words. Finally have each group work together to write text for the book, using words from their lists. Encourage students to include as many descriptive details as possible.
adapted from an idea by Marie Altenburg—Gr. 6, Lindenhurst Middle School, Lindenhurst, NY

Sidney: The Story Of A Kingfisher
written by John Mooy and Jane Stroschin
illustrated by Jane Stroschin
Henry Quill Press

Skill: Writing a personal narrative

In this lovely picture book, Sidney must learn to dive headfirst into the water to catch fish—but he's afraid. He tries different ways to catch fish, but none of them work for him. Finally Sidney develops the confidence to be himself and catch fish like a kingfisher. After I read this book to my students, we talk about skills we've gained through practice and perseverance (such as riding a bike and learning to ski). At the end of the discussion, I have each student write a personal narrative about a skill he has learned and become confident at doing. *Marian Kender—Gr. 6, St. Hugo Of The Hills School, Bloomfield Hills, MI*

The Pain And The Great One
written by Judy Blume
illustrated by Irene Trivas
Simon & Schuster Children's Books

Skill: Writing a personal narrative

To give students practice with writing personal narratives, I turn to Judy Blume's tale of sibling rivalry, *The Pain And The Great One*. First I tell students about my relationship with my own brother: even though we fought as kids, we still loved each other. Then I ask volunteers to share about their relationships with loved ones who sometimes annoy them. Next I read aloud *The Pain And The Great One*. I ask each student to think of a close friend or relative who also sometimes bothers her. Then I have the student write a paragraph describing how this person sometimes annoys her (without naming the person). In a second paragraph, the student gives reasons why she misses this person when he/she is not around. After students have finished writing, we discuss how similar we all are to the Pain and the Great One. *Michelle Sewing-Sohn—Media Specialist, Forest Park Elementary, Dix Hills, NY*

Miss Rumphius
written and illustrated by Barbara Cooney
The Viking Press

Skill: Writing a personal essay

Motivate students to look into their futures with this tale of a young girl who grows up to fulfill her life's mission: see the world, retire by the sea, and leave the world a nicer place. Read this gentle story aloud to your class; then ask each student to ponder his life's mission. Next have each student write a personal essay in which he shares about his life's mission. Encourage students to answer the five *W*s in their essays:

Whom do you hope to become?
What mission would you like to accomplish?
When would you like to accomplish this mission?
Where would you like to accomplish your mission?
Why would you like to accomplish this mission?

Bind the finished essays into a class book titled "Our Life Missions." Then watch as students take their first steps into the future—just by dreaming! *Patricia Twohey—Gr. 4, Old County Road School, Smithfield, RI*

Earrings!

written by Judith Viorst
illustrated by Nola Langner Malone
Atheneum

Skill: Persuasive writing

Give students practice in writing persuasively with this story about a girl trying to coerce her parents into letting her get her ears pierced. Begin by discussing times when students have tried to persuade their parents to give them something they really wanted. Then read *Earrings!* aloud to the class. After reading, list on the board the reasons the little girl gave her parents for allowing the piercing. Also discuss how she elaborated on each reason. Next have each child think of something he wants very badly. Then have him write a letter in which he tries to persuade a parent to give him what he wants. Remind students to elaborate on their reasons as the girl in the story did. You can bet you won't have to persuade students to finish this fun assignment! *La Tonne Leftwich—Gr. 4, Lake Dallas Elementary, Lake Dallas, TX*

What Makes A Picture Book Appealing?

Skill: Writing your own picture book

Before I have my students write their own picture books, we try to answer the question, "What makes a picture book appealing?" First I divide students into groups. Then I give each group several outstanding picture books. Each group reads its books together and discusses the characteristics that make them appealing (for example: easy-to-read text, interesting illustrations, good dialogue, colorful characters, etc.). As a class, we then create a list titled "Characteristics Of A Good Picture Book." I post this list in our classroom for students to refer to when they begin writing their own picture books. *Sharon Sobeck—Gr. 5, Saint Elizabeth Elementary, Pittsburgh, PA*

If You Give A Mouse A Cookie

written by Laura Joffe Numeroff
illustrated by Felicia Bond
Harpercollins Juvenile Books

Skill: Cause and effect

Provide practice with writing cause-and-effect statements with a story about a mouse who begins a comical chain of events simply by taking a cookie. After reading this book and Numeroff's follow-up, *If You Give A Moose A Muffin*, have each student fill in this sentence starter: "If you give a _____ a _____..." Then have the student use the starter to create a chain of events following Numeroff's pattern. Once the student has listed a chain of at least ten cause-and-effect statements, have her use them to write and illustrate her own picture book. Provide time for students to share their creations with a class of younger students. *Debbie Erickson, Waterloo Elementary, Waterloo, WI, and Leigh Taylor Bowman, David Youree Elementary, Smyrna, TN*

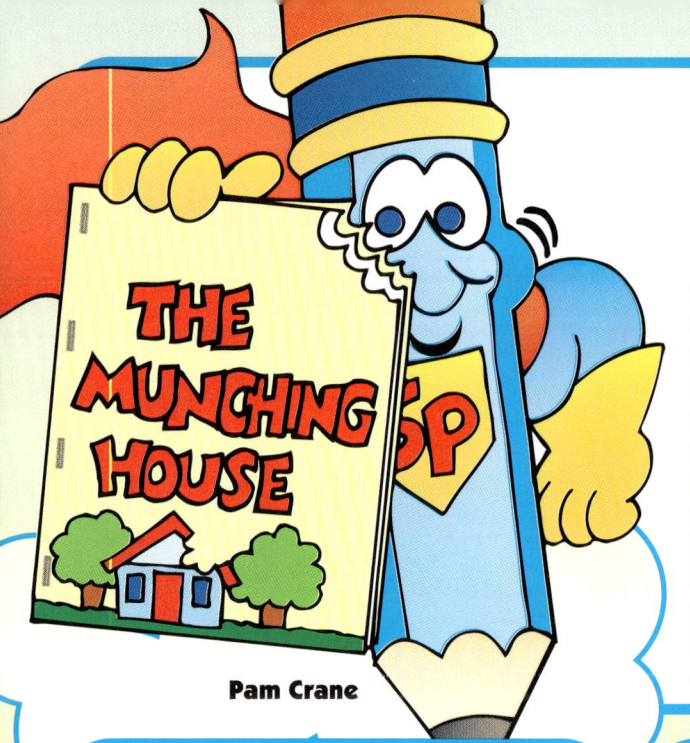
Pam Crane

The Napping House
written by Audrey Wood and illustrated by Don Wood
Harcourt Brace & Company

Skill: Using a thesaurus when writing

Find a good writer and you'll find a thesaurus close by! Teach students how to use this handy tool with Audrey Wood's delightful tale about a whole household asleep on a lazy afternoon. After reading the book aloud once, read it again, pointing out the synonyms for *sleeping*—such as "a *dreaming* child" and "a *dozing* dog." Then divide students into groups of four or five. Give each group a thesaurus and a card labeled with one of the following words: *eating, happy, sad, big, pretty, talking*. Have each student use a thesaurus to find two synonyms for his group's word; then have him create a sentence and illustration for each synonym. Have each team bind its pages together between a cover to create its own variation of *The Napping House* (i.e., "The Eating House," "The Happy House," etc.). *Diane M. Oswald—Librarian, Parkland Elementary, El Paso, TX*

Postcards From Pluto: A Tour Of The Solar System
written and illustrated by Loreen Leedy
Holiday House, Inc.

Skill: Writing nonfiction

Each year we combine our study of the solar system with a unit on writing nonfiction. After looking at several of *The Magic School Bus®* books, we discuss how author Joanna Cole presented factual information in a way that makes her books fun to read. We then read *Postcards From Pluto*. This charming book includes postcards written from children who are touring the planets. The postcards are creative, yet also contain factual information. After examining this book, each child chooses a planet to research and designs a postcard that includes at least six facts about the planet. As a follow-up, each student then creates her own nonfiction picture book about a topic of her choice. We conclude by reading our original picture books to other classes. What a great way to combine science, reading, and writing!
Michelle Discenza—Gr. 5
Morrisville Year-Round Elementary
Morrisville, NC

Will We Miss Them?: Endangered Species
written by Alexandra Wright
illustrated by Marshall Peck, III
Charlesbridge Publishing

Skill: Summarizing, writing a brief research report

Sharpen summarizing and report-writing skills with the help of a nonfiction picture book about endangered animals. After reading *Will We Miss Them?* aloud to the class, have each student research an endangered animal (ask your school's media specialist for a list or check the Internet). Then have the student write a brief summary of his animal, copying the format in *Will We Miss Them?:*

- a sentence that asks, "Will we miss the [name of animal]?"
- a paragraph that briefly describes the animal and its unique features
- a paragraph that tells why the animal is endangered and how it is currently being protected

Also have the student draw an illustration of his animal. Bind the finished pages together to make your own class version of this thought-provoking book. *Sherri Levitt—Gr. 4, Pembroke Elementary, Troy, MI*

Name _____ Story elements, writing a classificatory paper

It Takes Two!

Part 1: Choose two fiction picture books to compare. Read each book; then fill in the blanks below.

Title of Book #1: _____
Title of Book #2: _____

Theme: What did the main character learn by the end of the story? What was the author's main purpose in writing the book?

Book #1: _____

_____

Book #2: _____

_____

Setting: Where did the main action take place?

Book #1: _____

_____

Book #2: _____

_____

Characters: Who were the central characters in the story?

Book #1: _____

_____

Book #2: _____

_____

Plot: What happened to the main characters in the story?

Book #1: _____

_____

Book #2: _____

_____

Writing Style: What did you notice about the author's writing style? Was the author really good at describing things or people? Making you laugh? Writing dialogue?

Book #1: _____

_____

Book #2: _____

_____

Illustrations: What art medium was used? How did the pictures add to the story? Did the author also do the illustrations?

Book #1: _____

_____

Book #2: _____

_____

Part 2: On another sheet of paper, write a paragraph that tells how the two picture books are alike. Write a second paragraph that tells how the two books are different. Write a third paragraph that tells which book you liked best and why.

©2000 The Education Center, Inc. • *The Best Of* The Mailbox® *Writing* • *Intermediate* • TEC1485

Note To The Teacher: You may wish to have students complete this activity over several days.

Picture Books And Writing— A Dynamic Duo: Part 2

Using Picture Books To Teach Writing Skills

If you loved the picture books and writing unit featured on the preceding pages, then you're in luck! Here are even more of our readers' ideas for teaching key writing skills through picture books.

Earl's Too Cool For Me
written by Leah Komaiko and illustrated by Laura Cornell
Harper Trophy

Skill: Writing couplets

He rides a bicycle made of hay, knows several Martians personally, and even keeps monster eyes in jelly jars. That Earl—he's just too cool for me! At least that's what the little boy in this delightful picture book thinks. After reading this story to students, have each child write a two-line couplet about Earl (similar to those in the book), giving two new reasons why Earl is too cool. Have the student illustrate his couplet; then bind all of the students' pages into a class book. As an extension, challenge each student to write his own version of this book, substituting his own name for Earl's. Too cool! *Rita K. Wiebe—Gr. 4, Abraham Lincoln Elementary, Hastings, NE*

The Jester Has Lost His Jingle
written and illustrated by David Saltzman
The Jester Company, Inc.

Skill: Writing a persuasive paragraph

Author David Saltzman wrote this poignant book while a student at Yale University and after being diagnosed with Hodgkin's disease. In it, a happy-go-lucky Jester goes in search of laughter, which seems to be missing from the world. Begin by reading the Author's Note and the biographical information about Saltzman in the back of the book; then read the story aloud to your class. Ask students what they think Saltzman meant when he wrote about living the moment. Have students respond verbally or in their journals. Next share this statement: "A sense of humor is an important quality to possess." Have each student think about his opinion on this statement; then have him write a paragraph that states his opinion and tries to persuade the reader to agree with it. Remind students to give facts and examples to back up their opinions. *adapted from an idea by Merrill Watrous, Eugene, OR*

When I Was Young In The Mountains
written by Cynthia Rylant
illustrated by Diane Goode
E. P. Dutton, Inc.

Skill: Writing a biography

To introduce students to writing simple biographies, turn to this charming story by Cynthia Rylant. In it a young girl remembers her idyllic life tucked away in the mountains with her grandparents. After sharing the book with your class, have each student interview an older relative, neighbor, or friend about his/her life as a child. Then have the child use the information gathered in the interview to write a first-person biography about his interviewee titled "When I Was Young In _____." After final copies are finished, be sure to duplicate each story to send to its subject, along with a student-written thank-you note for the interview. *adapted from an idea by Ruth Howell—Gr. 4, Carlisle-Foster's Grove Elementary, Chesnee, SC*

The Wretched Stone
written and illustrated by Chris Van Allsburg
Houghton Mifflin Company

Skill: Narrative writing

In this captivating book by popular author and illustrator Chris Van Allsburg, a ship's crew finds a mysterious rock on an island and brings it aboard ship. Shortly afterward, the sailors begin to act strangely. What happens next is a surefire springboard for improving narrative-writing skills! After sharing this book with my class, we discuss the elements of a good narrative story. Then I pull out an unusual rock and show it to the class. I explain that I found it on my way to work and I wonder how it will affect our class. Next I challenge each student to write a narrative story about the rock, writing his tale in the format of a ship's log like in *The Wretched Stone*. Since students include each other in their stories, the interest level soars—along with their narrative-writing skills! *Michelle Bauml, Gladys Polk Elementary, Richwood, TX*

The Stinky Cheese Man And Other Fairly Stupid Tales
written by Jon Scieszka and illustrated by Lane Smith
Viking Press

Skill: Narrative writing, fairy tales

Talk about fractured fairy tales! More than a few twists are crammed into this hilarious takeoff on standard fairy tales. After studying the components of fairy tales (in conjunction with a unit on the Middle Ages), my students read a variety of fairy tales and compare the similar elements. Then I bring out *The Stinky Cheese Man...* book so students can see how traditional tales can be cleverly twisted. As a class we choose one fairy tale to rewrite as a group project. Enthusiasm builds as ideas and laughter reign! After this group effort, I challenge students to work alone or in small groups to create their own twisted tales. *Phyllis Ellett—Grs. 3 & 4, Earl Hanson School, Rock Island, IL*

Baseball Saved Us
written by Ken Mochizuki
illustrated by Dom Lee
Lee & Low Books Inc.

Skill: Narrative writing, research skills

Social studies, research skills, narrative writing: they're all between the pages of Ken Mochizuki's book set in a Japanese-American internment camp. After reading this stirring first-person story to students, brainstorm with them other historical events that might make a good basis for a similar story (for example, the signing of the Mayflower Compact, the Constitutional Congress, or the California Gold Rush). Have each student choose an event to research. Then have the student use the facts she gathers to write a narrative story—written in first person like *Baseball Saved Us*—based on the event. How's that for an activity that crosses your curriculum with ease? *Anita Perez—Gr. 5, Clyde Intermediate School, Clyde, TX*

A Chair For My Mother
written and illustrated by Vera B. Williams
Greenwillow Books

Skill: Writing a personal narrative

To introduce writing a personal narrative, I share with students this sweet story about a family that dreams of buying a new chair. After reading the book, I explain that it is an example of a personal narrative. I then post a chart listing the characteristics of a personal narrative:
- tells about a real experience
- features the author as the main character
- includes events told in sequence
- often includes dialogue
- includes rich details to help the reader visualize the experience

We then visit the media center where each child searches to find an example of a picture book that is a personal narrative. When we return to the classroom, I pair students so they can share their books. Partners use the chart as a checklist to determine if they have indeed selected books that are personal narratives. Finally we brainstorm a list of possible topics, and each child writes his own personal narrative story. *Michelle Discenza—Gr. 5, Morrisville Year-Round Elementary, Morrisville, NC*

Rosie's Walk
written and illustrated by Pat Hutchins
Simon & Schuster

Skill: Prepositional phrases, narrative writing

In this lively tale, a hen makes her way across the farmyard while a crafty fox tries to catch her for his dinner. After reading this book to students, I read it again, pointing out the prepositional phrases used throughout the story. Then I have each student write and illustrate her own book following the format of *Rosie's Walk*. The student must include at least five prepositional phrases and an animal protagonist. I award bonus points if a student also includes an antagonist like the fox. We share our finished books with the kindergarten and first-grade classes in our school. *Cheryl Case—Gr. 4, St. Martin North Elementary, Biloxi, MS*

Alexander And The Terrible, Horrible, No Good, Very Bad Day
written by Judith Viorst and illustrated by Ray Cruz
Atheneum

Skill: Writing a personal narrative

In this popular story, a little boy experiences one of *those* days, expressing his frustration as only a child can. After sharing this book with students, have each child create his own version, substituting his name in the title. Or have students shift gears and brainstorm elements that make for a fabulous day. Then have each child write a personal narrative story titled "My Exceptional, Terrific, Outstanding, Very Great Day!" *Leigh Taylor Bowman, David Youree Elementary, Smyrna, TN, and Melissa Goldenberg—Gr. 4, Oak Hill Elementary, Overland Park, KS*

Pam Crane

No Such Things
The Whingdingdilly
written and illustrated by Bill Peet
Houghton Mifflin Company

Skill: Descriptive writing

Populated with fantastic creatures, these two tales by Bill Peet are just the ticket for improving descriptive-writing skills. After reading the books aloud to students, have each child fold a sheet of drawing paper into thirds as shown. Direct the student to keep his paper folded and draw the head of an imaginary animal on the outside third. Then have the student pass his paper to a classmate so that the head is hidden from view. Have the second child add a body to the middle section without looking at the head; then have him fold the paper to reveal the unillustrated third section and pass the paper to another classmate. The last child adds a tail, then passes the paper back to the first student. Finally have each child write a descriptive paragraph or essay about his fantastic animal. Bind the completed descriptions and illustrations in a class book titled "Our Book Of No Such Things." *Cheryl Case—Gr. 4, St. Martin North Elementary, Biloxi, MS*

Wolf Stories

Skill: Classificatory writing, narrative writing, descriptive writing

Read a lot of fairy tales, and you're likely to bump into at least one big bad wolf! Let this furry fiend help your students sharpen a variety of writing skills. Ask your media center specialist to gather several versions of the fairy tale *The Three Little Pigs.* Share the books with students; then have each student write one classificatory paragraph that compares the wolves and another that contrasts them. Next have each student write his own story that includes a wolf character. Encourage the student to include lots of descriptive details about his wolf. Before you can huff or puff, your students' writing skills will be "grrrreat"! *Michele Kiel—Gr. 5, Woodside Elementary, Holland, MI*

Miss Rumphius
written and illustrated by Barbara Cooney
The Viking Press

Skill: Writing a personal essay

In this lovely story, Miss Rumphius decides at an early age to live a life that makes a difference in the world. After reading the book aloud, ask students, "What did Miss Rumphius think everyone should do in their lives?" *(Everyone should do something to make the world a better place.)* Then have each student list at least five things she can do to make her class, school, home, or community a better place. After lists are completed, have each student choose one or two items from her list to act on in the next two weeks. At the end of the two-week period, have each student write a personal essay telling how she felt doing the activity (activities) and what results she saw. Students are sure to see there's more than one way to make a difference! *Gail Peckumn, Jefferson, IA*

Name _____ Narrative writing, point of view

If I Had My Way,...

Books—good ones, that is—are full of great characters who seem to jump off the page. Well, what if a character jumped off the page of the picture book you just read? What would he/she have to say about how the author wrote the story? How would the character rewrite the book? What suggestions would the character give the author?

Directions: Pretend that you are a character from a picture book you have read. Think about that character's personality. Then, in the speech bubble, write about how you would change the book's plot. Include suggestions you would give the author to improve the book. In the box, draw a picture of the character.

Picture Book: _____

Author: _____

Character: _____

Bonus Box: Which character in this story would probably be most pleased with how the author wrote the book? Write and explain your answer on the back of this page.

©2000 The Education Center, Inc. • *The Best Of The Mailbox® Writing • Intermediate* • TEC1485

Note To The Teacher: Provide each student group with an assortment of picture books to read before completing this page. Also use this reproducible as a book-report project or as a writing activity for a novel your class is reading.

Writing Workshop WISDOM

Teacher-Tested Tips And Activities From Our Subscribers

It's ten o'clock and time for your students' daily writing workshop. How can you make the most of this important instructional period? What writing activities will motivate the student who never seems to want to write about anything? Wise up about writing workshop with these classroom-tested tips and ideas from our subscribers.

TIPS

Call The "COPS"!

Want to make sure your students proofread their work one more time before turning it in? Call in the "COPS"! When one of my students finishes a piece, he must write COPS lightly across the top of his paper. This step reminds him to:
- proofread for **capitalization**; then cross off the C.
- proofread for **overall appearance**; then cross off the O.
- proofread for **punctuation**; then cross off the P.
- proofread for **spelling**; then cross off the S.

This simple reminder is an easy way to reinforce the important step of proofreading.
Diana A. Hoffman—Gr. 6, Chase Middle School, Topeka, KS

Sponge Art Book Covers

When a student is ready to publish his written work, show him this easy tip for producing a stunning cover. Press the large tip of a triangular makeup sponge on a stamp pad. Next press the sponge along the edge of a piece of paper, always pressing at the corner of the sponge. Continue dabbing the tip of the sponge over the paper, turning the sponge slightly each time to create a three-dimensional effect. Write the title of the story and author's name in the center of the paper.
*Michelle Bourlet—Grs. 4–6, Tabernacle Baptist School
Clayton, GA*

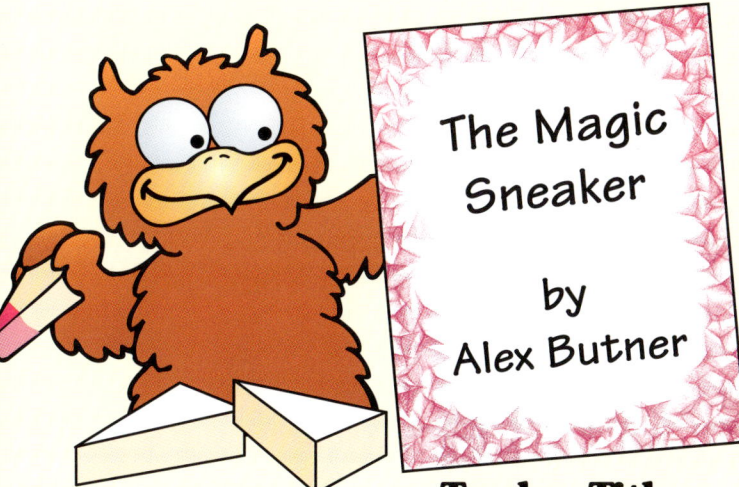

Twelve Titles

My school holds a first-day orientation, attended by both parents and students. On this day, I give each parent (unbeknownst to his or her child) a sheet of paper entitled "A Dozen Terrific Titles For Unwritten Stories." I ask the parent to list 12 titles for stories his or her child could write this year. (Ask another staff member to write a list for a student whose parent can't attend.) I file these lists in each student's portfolio.

At our first writing workshop, I surprise each child with his list of titles. Students love the idea of using titles provided by their parents. Plus I discover a lot about my kids' hobbies, families, and interests through their parents' titles. We bind all of the finished stories together in personal writing booklets to share with parents at conference time or Open House.
Mary E. Sullivan—Gr. 4, Nichols School, Monona, WI

21

Highlighting Helper

When my students conference with me during writing workshop, they often share stories in which information has been poorly organized. I use colored highlighters to help a student arrange his thoughts more clearly. Using a different color for each paragraph, we highlight information that should be grouped together. The student can then rewrite his piece independently, putting information that has been highlighted in the same color in the same paragraph.
Deborah Howard—Gr. 4, Bellows Free Academy, Fairfax, VT

A Schoolwide Writing Process

Several years ago our school staff determined a specific series of writing process steps to use schoolwide. Each teacher made a poster of the process steps to display in her classroom. This small step provides a sense of continuity that gives our student writers a greater measure of confidence in their writing.
Debbie Easterday—Gr. 4, Skyview Elementary Thornton, CO

Keeping Writers On Task

Keeping everyone focused during writing workshop can sometimes be a challenge. To encourage my students to stay on task, I carry a small notebook in which I've labeled a page for each child. At an unannounced time, I silently observe each child; then I draw a star on the page of each student who is working on task. At the end of the grading period, I use the stars to determine participation grades for writing workshop. The notebook also comes in handy at conference time.
Debbie Easterday—Gr. 4

The Sandwich Theory

The third step in my writing workshop is *peer conferencing*. When one of my students has written his rough draft, he must find two classmates who will listen to his story with an ear for its content. As a group of three, the students work through what I call the Sandwich Theory. The first step (the top piece of bread) reminds peer editors to list a few positive notes about the piece so that they can start the conference on an uplifting note. The middle of the sandwich (the meat) tells peer editors to list helpful suggestions so the author can improve his work. The third step (the last piece of bread) reminds editors to close the conference with another positive note summarizing the piece's best points. The author—now ready for the revision stage—takes these encouraging and helpful notes back to his desk and starts refining his work.
Linda Stroik—Gr. 4, Jackson Elementary, Stevens Point, WI

PEER EDITORS:
Begin with a positive comment.
List helpful suggestions.
End with a positive comment.
Don't Forget The Sandwich Theory!

Experts In Residence

In my class, students help each other through every step of writing workshop. Besides helping one another brainstorm ideas and editing each other's work, my kids also serve as "experts in residence." For example, more artistic students have become "illustrators in residence," helping classmates illustrate their work. Other students are "playwrights in residence," assisting classmates in converting their work into skits or plays. This spirit of cooperation is a great addition to our writing workshop!
Kathy Guyer—Gr. 5, Dover Elementary, Dover, PA

Peer-Editing Tip

Divide and conquer—that's the motto behind this peer-editing tip. During writing workshop, require that each student ask three different peers to edit his work. Have one peer edit for spelling errors, one for punctuation and usage, and one for readability (i.e., "Does this make sense?"). The author makes sure that each editor signs off on his paper, indicating which editing role he played. *(For a terrific peer-editing checklist, see the reproducible on page 25.)*
Anne Runyon—Grs. 4/5, Littleton, CO

Managing Writing Workshop

Because of writing workshop's emphasis on individualized learning, my students are continually working on different steps of the writing process. To monitor each child's progress, I designed a management chart that lists the six steps of the writing process (see the illustration). I also labeled a pinch clothespin for each child in my class. At the beginning of the workshop, each student clips his clothespin to the chart, indicating the step he'll be working on that day. At a glance, I can tell who will be working independently, with a peer, or with me.
Kathy Guyer—Gr. 5, Dover Elementary, Dover, PA

Unit Pretests

Because I was having a difficult time covering both English and creative-writing skills in my writing workshop, I started to pretest each English unit. The pretest helps me to group my students during writing workshop. For example, if a student showed mastery on the quotation marks pretest, he works on a creative-writing project during writing workshop; students who need additional instruction on quotation marks meet with me for a skill lesson before starting on their creative-writing piece. Using pretests allows me to zero in on students who need more intensive skills instruction.
*Julie Oliver—Gr. 6,
Jones Cove School, Cosby, TN*

WRITING ACTIVITIES

Lost And Found

Lost for an ingenious writing activity for today's writing workshop? Head to the office to retrieve your school's Lost and Found box. Have each student choose an item from the box, study it, and then write an outline for a story about the missing article:

    Who lost the item?
    When was the item lost?
    Where was the item lost?
    Under what circumstances was the item lost?
    How has the loss of the item affected its owner?

After the outlines are completed, have each student write a story about his lost object. Or have students pretend to be their missing articles and write first-person accounts about being lost.
Julia Alarie—Gr. 6, Essex Middle School, Essex, VT

This Is Your Life!

Your next writing workshop topic may be sitting right on your kids' desks! Have each student pick up his pencil and examine it for three minutes, jotting down details. As a class, have students brainstorm about the experiences an average pencil might go through in a normal day: copying homework assignments, being sharpened, erasing a math error, landing on the floor ten times, etc. Have students use this list and their imaginations to write stories entitled "My Life As A Pencil." Other classroom objects that are perfect subjects for a "This Is My Life" story include a chair, a chalkboard, a lunchbox, a hall pass—even the teacher's bookbag!
Debbie Scott—Grs. 4–6, Miller Road Baptist Academy, Garland, TX

Fold And Pass, Please!

When students complain, "I can't think of anything to write about," try this fun prewriting activity. Have each student write the name of an interesting character (fictional or nonfictional) at the top of her paper; then have her fold down the top of the paper to conceal what she's written and pass it to the next person on her team or row. That student adds another character to the paper, folds the paper to conceal what he's written, and passes it once again. The next two students repeat the process, adding a setting and an intriguing situation/plot twist. After papers have been returned to their original owners, students unfold them to reveal the story elements they'll use during writing workshop. Your kids will love the challenge of creating interesting story elements for their classmates!
Julie Plowman—Gr. 6, Adair-Casey Elementary, Adair, IA

Kiddie Lit For Big Kids

One of my sixth graders' favorite writing-workshop activities proves that picture books aren't just for little readers. I begin the workshop by reading a popular picture book, *If You Give A Mouse A Cookie* by Laura J. Numeroff. After reading the book, I challenge each of my students to write and illustrate his own picture book using Numeroff's book as a model. We brainstorm a list of possibilities to help students who are suffering from a mild case of writer's block; then each child chooses an idea and develops a story around it. After the books are finished, my students share them with a kindergarten class. Now that's writing with a purpose! *Julie Plowman—Gr. 6*

A Cure For Writer's Block

Writer's block—it's not a very pleasant street to be on if you're sitting in writing workshop! When one of my students is having a difficult time generating a writing topic, I give her this starter: "Here I sit in writing workshop, unable to think of anything to write about. I'd really rather be…." The student then proceeds to write about the thing(s) she'd rather be doing and the place(s) she'd rather be sitting! Bye-bye, writer's block!
Janet Smith—Gr. 5, Meade Memorial Elementary, Williamsport, KY

Peer-Editing Conference Form

Writer: _____   Peer Editor: _____

1. Is this draft neat enough to be easily read? **NO   YES**
   If NO, how could it be made neater and easier to read? _____
   _____
   _____

2. List the words that you think are misspelled. If you need more space, use the back of this page.
   _____   _____
   _____   _____
   _____   _____
   _____   _____

   PROOFREADING SYMBOLS

Symbol	Meaning
∧	Insert a letter, word, phrase, or sentence.
sp	Check the spelling.
ꭥ	Take out a letter, word, phrase, or sentence.
≡	Change a small letter to a capital letter.
∧,	Insert a comma.
/	Change a capital letter to a small letter.
⊙	Insert a period.
ᵛᵛ ᵛᵛ	Insert quotation marks.
¶	Begin and indent a new paragraph.

3. Is this story written in the correct order or sequence?   **NO   YES**   If NO, how could this problem be corrected? _____
   _____

4. Are the following story elements explained in enough detail? (Circle YES or NO.)
   • the main character **NO   YES**   If NO, how could the character be explained better?
   _____
   _____

   • the setting (when and where the story takes place)   **NO   YES**   If NO, how could the setting be explained better? _____
   _____

   • the plot or main idea   **NO   YES**   If NO, how could the plot or main idea be explained better? _____
   _____

   • the main conflict or problem in the story   **NO   YES**   If NO, how could the conflict be explained better? _____
   _____

   • the solution to the conflict   **NO   YES**   If NO, how could the solution be explained better?
   _____
   _____

5. On the back of this paper, list three things you liked about this paper.

©2000 The Education Center, Inc. • *The Best Of* The Mailbox® *Writing* • Intermediate • TEC1485

Note To Teacher: Use this reproducible with the writing workshop tips on pages 21–24.

You Oughta Be In ~~Pictures~~ Print!
Terrific Tips For Classroom Publishing

All the *t*'s are crossed and the *i*'s are dotted. The penmanship is marvelous, and the margins are just right. Now what do you do with all those wonderful writings your students have produced? These practical tips from our savvy subscribers are all you need to turn your classroom into a publishing center!

Barry Slate

Small Presses

Small literary presses are very receptive to young writers. I have an arrangement with a small literary press to publish some of my class' work. Imagine the looks on my students' faces when they see their poems, short stories, and even artwork appear on the pages of a small-press magazine! Most bookstores have references about small presses, such as *The International Directory Of Little Magazines And Small Presses* published by Dustbooks. When contacting a company, include a brief introductory letter, along with samples of your students' writings. You'll usually receive a positive response! *Michael H. Brownstein, Chicago, IL*

A Book About My Buddy

Buddy up with a primary class for a publishing project that will make your students eager to put pencil to page. My fifth graders brainstormed eight to ten interview questions to ask first-grade children. Questions pertained to age, family, home, pets, friends, hobbies, and future goals. After agreeing on guidelines, we chose the top seven questions, with each student adding one more of his own. I then obtained a first-grade class roster and assigned each student a young buddy to interview. Upon completing an interview, each student wrote a book about his buddy using one page for each interview question. Students shared their ideas with each other and partners proofread one another's work. I made further corrections before students began rewriting their final copies. Students drew illustrations or added magazine and catalog pictures. The books were neatly printed by hand or typed on a computer; then they were presented to the younger children during a "read-aloud get-together" in our school gym. How's that for publishing with a purpose? *Marcia Smith—Grs. 4–5, Washington Elementary, Circleville, OH*

Big Book Construction Company

A primary teacher, having difficulty finding suitable reading materials about the Wild West for her students, challenged my writing class to create big books for her. First my students formed cooperative groups and examined some big books. Each student then wrote a Wild West story and shared it with his classmates. Using criteria that they had developed, students chose five stories to publish. Our own "publishing companies" revised and edited the stories. A final copy of each one was written and used for the general layout of the big book.

Students used ten-foot-long pieces of bulletin-board paper to create their big books. Sides were folded over to reinforce the thickness of each page; then the paper was accordion-folded. (See the illustration.) Job assignments included chief illustrators, assistant illustrators, calligraphers, materials managers, and advisors. Because bulletin-board paper was used, students could work simultaneously on different pages when the book was fully extended. Little books were also made to correlate with the big books. These were high-quality, semi-hardback versions with illustrations. The primary students used the little books, along with an audiocassette, at listening centers. What an unforgettable learning experience—for both classes! *Janet Smith—Grs. 5–6, Meade Elementary, Williamsport, KY*

Creating Cartoon Books

Looking for a quick and effective publishing activity? It's right in the funny pages! My students love to make cartoon books. After clipping out regular newspaper cartoon strips, we cut the panels apart and snip off the conversation bubbles. Each panel is glued to a four-inch square of paper; then students add their own dialogue. When the panels are completed, a title page is placed on top and all of the pages are stapled together. Each child then has his own unique cartoon book to read and share. Now wasn't that easy? *Sonya Franklin, Auburn, AL*

Fold-Out Books

My students enjoy making timelines about their lives. A fold-out book is an excellent way to turn a timeline into a published product. First cut 12" x 18" sheets of white paper into 4" x 18" strips. Give each child three strips. (More can be provided if needed.) Have each child glue the strips end to end to make one long strip. With a ruler, have him divide the strip into four-inch squares, lightly penciling in the divisions and trimming any excess.

Now it's time to begin writing. In the first square, the student includes his birthdate, some brief comments, and an illustration. The timeline is continued in sequence on the other squares. Personal, national, or world events, along with their dates, can also be included. Have each student make a 4 1/2" x 10" cover from tagboard, folding it so that there's a one-half-inch spine. After illustrating and titling his cover, have each student glue the first square of his timeline to the inside back cover. He then accordion-folds the remaining pages. Display the books atop library shelves where everyone can enjoy them! *Betty Adams—Gr. 5, Staunton Elementary, Staunton, IN*

Appetizing Adjectives

After a lesson on adjectives, I shared some restaurant menus with my class. We discussed what made the food on the menus seem so appetizing. We also compared the restaurant menus with school menus. I then cut apart several old school menus and had each child randomly choose a meal. The student's task was to use adjectives to describe her meal so that it would appeal to the world's pickiest eater. Students glued pictures or drawings of their meals on white paper; then they copied their revised menus below the illustrations. All of the pages were bound between a front and back cover. We shared our class book with the cafeteria staff. They loved it! *Kathy Bray—Gr. 4, West School, Carlinville, IL*

Parts Of Speech—Animalia Style

I use Graeme Base's wonderful picture book *Animalia* to teach dictionary, vocabulary, and parts-of-speech skills. My students cooperatively write their own versions of the book—a project they enjoy so much they don't even realize they're learning! First read *Animalia* aloud to your class. Point out all of the pictures—within each whole picture—that start with the same letter. When finished, introduce the literary term *alliteration*. Discuss the pattern of the text, which is mostly *adjective-adjective-noun-adverb-verb-adjective-noun*. Working in pairs, have students use dictionaries to find interesting words to create their own text using Base's pattern. When the text is completed, have students add illustrations. Encourage students to use lots of pictures that illustrate words beginning with their alphabet letters. Although this project may take awhile to complete, your students will love it. *Ronda Nissen—Gr. 4, Spring Bluff School, Winthrop Harbor, IL*

Illustration Center

A picture's worth a thousand words, so teach your students how to use illustrations as a tool when writing. I make sure that my art center is well supplied with stencils, markers, scissors, crayons, construction paper, fine-tipped markers, stickers, and colored pencils. These resources are available to students for the illustrating phase of their writing. When my young writers get "writer's block," I suggest that they concentrate on the illustrations to generate further ideas. *Maxine Pincott—Gr. 4, Oliver Ellsworth School, Windsor, CT*

Donating Published Works

My students enjoyed writing, editing, illustrating, printing, and publishing their own books. We then donated them to our public library, where they became a permanent part of the books in circulation. The books have been so popular that there's a waiting list to check them out. My students feel like "real" authors! *Michelle Bourlet—Grs. 4-6, Tabernacle Baptist School, Clayton, GA*

Maintaining Portfolios

Each student in my class has a writer's notebook, which serves as a personal writing portfolio. Each time a child finishes a piece of writing, he mounts it on a piece of paper, punches holes in the paper, and stores it in his notebook. A publishing center in our classroom is equipped with glue, scissors, paper, a hole punch, and other materials necessary for creating pages for the notebooks. Students enjoy the independence and sense of accomplishment of maintaining their own writing portfolios. *Linda Maxwell, Edgewood School, Birmingham, AL*

The Friendship Book

To promote self-esteem, positive thinking, and creative writing, my students make friendship books. Each student draws the name of a classmate from a hat. He then writes a complimentary story about that person. The stories are always very creative. The subject is sometimes a hero who saves a family from a burning building, someone with supernatural powers, an Olympic athlete, a millionaire, the president of the United States, or a successful doctor who discovers a miracle drug. Some stories are true ones in which acts of kindness are described. After the stories are edited and illustrated, we have a "Friendship Day" and share the stories aloud. The kids love hearing about themselves. Each story is then bound as a book, complete with a laminated cover. At the end of the year, each student receives the book written about himself or herself. *Lisa Myers—Gr. 5, Wendell GT Magnet Elementary, Wendell, NC*

Clothesline Creations

Hang around my classroom long enough and you'll read some pretty imaginative stories—all written on articles of clothing made from construction paper and other art materials. My students have written stories on cut-out overalls, shirts, blue jeans, dresses, hats, cheer-leading skirts, and tuxedos. One of my students even wrote a romance story on a paper wedding dress! We hang the "clothes" with clothespins from a clothesline that is stretched across the classroom. Students really get excited about reading their classmates' tales and seeing the variety of clothes that have been created. *Lisa Ware—Gr. 5, North Jackson Elementary, Talmo, GA*

Writing Picture Books

A book-writing unit is an important component of my district's sixth-grade reading program. First the students review several types of preschool through second-grade reading materials. From these materials, each student determines the reading level and type of book that he or she wants to write. A rough sketch of the book, including all the text and art, is then completed. After editing their writings, students make final copies. The pages are laminated and hand-sewn together. Students have produced alphabet books, counting books, and all types of storybooks. One young author wrote a book for her little sister entitled *If You Give My Sister Crayons,* which was based on the picture book favorite *If You Give A Mouse A Cookie.* To culminate the project, the books are shared in our home economics classes during a child care unit; then they are read to classes in a local elementary school. *Louise S. Johnson—Gr. 6, Adams Middle School, Trenton, MO*

Real Publishing

Stone Soup is a magazine that features writings and artwork by young people under the age of 14. I keep copies in my classroom, read aloud from them, and make them available to students to read on their own. I also tell students about The National Written & Illustrated By...Awards Contest For Students. This publishing contest is open to young people (ages 6–19), with a yearly deadline of May 1. To build excitement, I read to students the works of previous winners.

To receive a copy of the contest rules and guidelines, send a self-addressed, stamped envelope to The National Written & Illustrated By...Awards Contest For Students, Landmark Editions, Inc., P.O. Box 270169, Kansas City, MO 64127. *Kay Lents—Gr. 5, Marshalltown, IA*

Worthy Of Xeroxing

There's something about having a Xeroxed copy that makes a student's writing seem *really* published. On a weekly basis, I allow each of my students to choose one written item to put in my "Worthy Of Xeroxing" box. On Friday, I duplicate the papers so that students can take copies home to share. If a paper is especially well written, I make two copies and place one in our special Class Book. *Shirley Gillette—Chapter I Reading, Lafe Nelson School, Safford, AZ*

Books On Publishing

From the conception of an idea to techniques for binding books, the following are valuable resources for young authors:

Making Books: A Step-By-Step Guide To Your Own Publishing by Gillian Chapman and Pam Robson, Millbrook Press Trade

The Art Of The Handmade Book by Flora Fennimore, Chicago Review Press

If You Were A Writer by Joan Lowery Nixon, Four Winds Press

Awesome Author Day

Searching for a new way to share students' writings? Try an Awesome Author Day! Each six weeks, our fourth graders eagerly meet in the cafeteria for a special time of sharing their original writings. One at a time, the students come to the microphone to read their prose, poetry, plays, and stories. While waiting to take their turns to read, other classes listen attentively. This special occasion provides an extra incentive for everyone to complete an original writing in time for the next Awesome Author Day. *Lynne Moore—Gr. 4, Jennie Reid Elementary, La Porte, TX*

Bookplates

Reproduce these bookplates for students to attach to the inside front covers of products that they publish. Have students carefully fill in the blanks, then use glue to attach the plates to their books.

This book,
_____,
was written
&
illustrated
by
_____
on
_____.

Award

Reproduce this award to honor students' writing accomplishments.

The Spotlight's On You Because You've Been Published!

This award is presented to

_____
(writer)

by

_____
(chief editor)

_____
(date)

©2000 The Education Center, Inc.

Presenting...
Paragraph Pointers
Teaching Students How To Write Good Paragraphs

The pen may be mightier than the sword—but if your students don't know how to compose a good paragraph, their writing will be anything but mighty. Point the way to more proficient paragraph writing with the following fun activities and reproducibles.

by Becky Andrews

The Sandwich Technique

With one captivating demonstration, you can teach your students to construct a paragraph just as easily as they might make a sandwich. Set up a table at the front of the room; then load it with several different sandwich ingredients. Begin by asking, "What two things are going to hold my sandwich together?" Students should reply that two slices of bread are necessary. Put the two slices together and ask, "Is my sandwich ready to eat?" Even the pickiest eater will soundly reply, "NO!" Then ask, "What will make my sandwich more interesting?" Lead students to conclude that different ingredients will make the sandwich interesting. Put a leaf of lettuce between the bread slices and ask, "Is this one ingredient enough to make the sandwich interesting?" Continue by letting students suggest different ingredients to put in your sandwich.

What does this demonstration have to do with paragraphs? Draw the diagram shown on the chalkboard. Explain to students that, like a sandwich, a good paragraph needs two things to hold it together: a *topic sentence* to start the paragraph and a *conclusion* to end it. A good paragraph also needs several details that support, explain, or prove the topic sentence. These details, like a sandwich's ingredients, are placed in the middle and make the paragraph interesting. Once students have grasped this real-life analogy, they're ready for the activities that follow.

Details, Details, Details

Utilize the cards found on pages 41 and 42 to help your students list details for a good paragraph. Duplicate a copy of each page. Then color and cut the cards apart and place them in a bag. Then use them in one of the following activities:

- Have a volunteer draw a card from the bag. Write the topic sentence from the card at the top of the chalkboard; then write the conclusion at the bottom. Have students suggest details that would "fit" in the middle. Remind them to stick to the topic and try to select details that will prove, explain, or support the topic sentence. After writing three to five details on the board (in between the topic sentence and conclusion), divide the class into pairs or cooperative groups. Have each group write a paragraph using the sentences on the board. Provide time for groups to share their completed paragraphs.

- Divide your class into cooperative groups. Give each group a card. Have the group list five details for the topic on its card, then write a finished paragraph. By rotating the cards from group to group, your students will have plenty of practice gathering details, details, and more details.

- For additional practice on writing details, see the reproducible worksheets on pages 34–36.

Writing Topic Sentences

"But what do I write about?" Eliminate this pesky question by teaching students how to write their own topic sentences. Try these surefire activities:

- Explain that a good paragraph starts with a specific topic or idea, which is stated in a *topic sentence.* Have the class brainstorm a list of broad topics such as homework, parents, school, cats, best friends, cars, pizza, football, etc. After listing at least ten topics, have students choose one, such as school. Brainstorm a list of specific ideas about school that could be used as topic sentences. For example, "Math is an important subject" or "Our school is a good place to learn about computers." Continue choosing general topics from your list and writing two or three topic sentences for each.

- Write each word below on a construction-paper card. Place the cards in a bag. Divide the class into pairs; then have each pair draw a card from the bag. Instruct each pair to write two topic sentences for the topic on its card. After sharing their topic sentences, have teams write each of their topic sentences on an index card. Collect the cards; then use them whenever you need a quick topic for students to write about.

cats	drugs	our town	cars	little sisters (or brothers)
the beach	poetry	skateboards	rap music	money
my house	vegetables	space travel	night	jobs
teachers	recess	homework	junk food	movies

- For more topic sentence ideas, duplicate a copy of the "Digging Up A Good Idea" reproducible on page 39. Have students staple copies inside their writing folders for a ready supply of paragraph topics. Also duplicate one copy of the checklist on page 40 for each student. Have students place the checklist in their folders to use as a reference. Use additional copies to help students organize their paragraphs in the activities that follow.

Writing Descriptive Paragraphs

Now that students know how to construct a good paragraph, how can you motivate them to write more descriptively than "It was a nice day"? Use the following ideas to encourage more exact and colorful writing:

- A field trip for writing paragraphs? That's right! Tell students that they will soon be going on a special field trip. But before they can leave, they will need some special equipment. Divide your class into three cooperative groups. Then give one group a pair of earmuffs. Explain that this group will be the "ears" of the class. Give another group a pair of glasses or binoculars, explaining that it will be the "eyes." Pass a can of air freshener to another group, designating it as the "nose" of the class. Head to a special place in your school, such as the cafeteria, library, gym, or playground. Instruct each group to make as many observations about its topic (sounds, sights, smells) as possible. Back in the room, write the following headings on the board, leaving space after each one for three to five details:

    What would a person who visited this place see?
    What would a person who visited this place hear?
    What would a person who visited this place smell?

  Challenge each group to list three to five details for its particular topic. Encourage students to use details that are so specific that a reader would easily be able to imagine what they are describing. For example, instead of "There were a lot of cooks standing over the pot of spaghetti," say, "Three or four red-faced cooks stood over the steaming pot of spaghetti." After listing the details on the board, have each group write a paragraph on its topic.

- For additional descriptive writing practice, see the reproducible worksheet on page 37.

Writing Narrative Paragraphs

Kids (and adults) love to tell stories about themselves. But writing about a personal experience can often be difficult for young writers. The middle part often ends up being told first while the beginning is explained after the ending. To illustrate the importance of telling the events of a story in order, invite a faculty member—principal, school secretary, cafeteria manager, custodian—to tell students a brief story about his or her most embarrassing moment. (Prior to the talk, be sure to remind the speaker about telling the story in sequence.) Follow this talk by telling your own tale about an embarrassing moment; but unlike the previous speaker, scramble the order of events as you talk. After the talk, ask students, "Which story made more sense and was easier to follow?" Explain that they must keep the events in order when they write a paragraph that tells about something that happened to them.

Next distribute copies of the reproducible worksheet on page 38. Provide time for students to add paragraphs and illustrations to their booklets. Put the finished booklets in a large basket to be placed in your reading center. These booklets will be hot properties in no time!

Writing An Opinion Paragraph

Ask a kid his opinion on a topic that's important to him, and you're likely get an enthusiastic response! But writing an opinion and giving one verbally are two different things. To help your students write good opinion paragraphs try these activities:

- Write the following statements on the board:
  Our school's basketball team is better than yours.
  Our school's basketball team won more games than any other school in the city this year.

  Ask students to identify the *fact* (a statement that can be proven as definitely true or false) and the *opinion* (someone's personal idea about the topic). Then ask which statement would be more effective in a paragraph about the success of your school's basketball team. Since opinions don't prove anything, facts make better details than opinions. Continue practice with these pairs of statements:

  Olivia is the best artist in school.
  Olivia has won all three art contests this year.

  He's not working very hard on this project.
  He didn't turn in his assignments on Monday or Tuesday.

  Skateboarding is dangerous.
  Three children were injured this month while riding skateboards.

- Divide your class into cooperative teams. Hold up a magazine picture of a famous person such as Michael Jordan. Have each group write one fact and one opinion about the person. List all of the facts on one side of the board and all of the opinions on the other. Then ask, "If I were going to write a paragraph about the success of Michael Jordan, which details would get that point across best?" Students should conclude that facts make more effective details than opinions do in getting a point across.

- Get your students to write opinion paragraphs by listing these topic sentences on the board. Individually, in pairs, or in groups, have students first list facts to support each topic sentence; then have them write their facts in the form of a paragraph. There will be some lively debates when these paragraphs are shared!

  Every child should (or should not) have a pet.
  It's important (or unimportant) to be popular.
  Children under the age of five should (or should not) be allowed to watch music videos.
  It would be great (or terrible) to be a school principal.
  Children should (or should not) be paid for doing chores at home.

FACTS
- He played on a championship team in college.
- He won many basketball awards.
- He played basketball in the Olympics.
- He has won slam-dunk contests.
- His team won the NBA Championship.

OPINIONS
- He is fun to watch on television.
- He is better than Magic Johnson.
- He is a good player.
- He is the best basketball player in the world.
- There is no player better than him.

Michael Jordan is a great basketball player.

Name _____   Paragraphs: basic structure

Don't Forget The Details!

A paragraph is a lot like a sandwich. It has two main parts that hold it together, just like the two slices of bread that hold a sandwich together. The beginning of a paragraph is called the *topic sentence*. The topic sentence tells what the paragraph is about. The ending is called the *conclusion*. It restates the topic sentence.

In between the topic sentence and the conclusion are the *details*. Details are sentences that prove, explain, or support the topic given in your topic sentence. Just like you can't build a good sandwich without ingredients to put between the bread, you can't build a good paragraph without interesting details.

Directions: Fill in the blanks with details for each topic sentence. Use the back of this sheet if you need additional space.

A good friend has a variety of qualities.

a. _____
b. _____
c. _____
d. _____
e. _____

Friendship is made up of many things.

Baby-sitting can be a hard job.

a. _____
b. _____
c. _____
d. _____
e. _____

Sometimes it is difficult being a baby-sitter.

Playing on a sports team is good for a kid.

a. _____
b. _____
c. _____
d. _____
e. _____

There are good reasons to play team sports.

There are some unusual commercials on television today.

a. _____
b. _____
c. _____
d. _____
e. _____

Some television commercials are very unusual.

Now choose one of the four topics. On the back of this sheet or on another piece of paper, write your own paragraph using the topic sentence, details, and conclusion listed above.

Name _____   Paragraphs: listing details

Spotlight On Kids

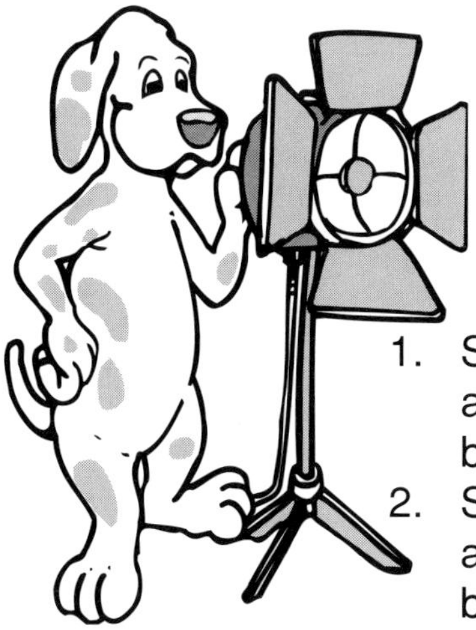

Below are some topic sentences about a very important subject—KIDS! Write two details for each topic sentence. Remember that details should prove, explain, or support the topic sentence.

1. Senior citizens can be a big help to kids.
   a. _____
   b. _____
2. Some fads and fashions are popular with today's kids.
   a. _____
   b. _____
3. A kid can do several things every day to be a good student.
   a. _____
   b. _____
4. It was a day this kid will never forget!
   a. _____
   b. _____
5. Do you want to know how parents can get kids to clean their rooms?
   a. _____
   b. _____

On the lines below, write a paragraph about one of the topic sentences. Begin your paragraph with the topic sentence. Add at least three details. End your paragraph with a conclusion that restates your topic sentence. Use the back of this sheet if you need more space.

_____
_____
_____
_____
_____
_____
_____
_____
_____
_____
_____
_____
_____
_____
_____
_____

Bonus Box: Can kids your age make a difference in the world today? Choose a problem that concerns you. On the back of this sheet, list at least three things that kids like you can do to solve the problem.

©2000 The Education Center, Inc. • *The Best Of* The Mailbox® *Writing* • Intermediate • TEC1485

Name _____ Paragraphs: listing details

Same Topic, Different Idea

These topic sentences are both about the same thing—dogs. But because the ideas are different, the details must be different too.

Topic sentences	Details
Dogs make great pets.	would tell or list reasons why dogs make great pets
Dogs can be useful to people.	would explain or list ways that dogs are useful to people

Directions: For each topic sentence, decide what kind of details you would need to prove, explain, or support the sentence. Write your answer in the blanks.

1. **Homework is important.**
   Details would _____

2. **Homework should not be assigned on weekends.**
   Details would _____

3. **Kids can earn money in several ways.**
   Details would _____

4. **Money is different around the world.**
   Details would _____

5. **I'll never forget one family vacation.**
   Details would _____

6. **Too many family vacations can be hazardous to your health!**
   Details would _____

7. **Kids today have hobbies that are very different from those their parents enjoyed.**
   Details would _____

8. **Stamp collecting is a fascinating hobby.**
   Details would _____

Bonus Box: Unscramble this topic sentence: malls are fun shopping. On the back of this sheet, write the sentence; then write what kind of details you would need in a paragraph about the topic sentence.

Name _____

Paragraphs: writing descriptive paragraphs

"It's Just Like You Described It!"

Get ready to take a trip like you've never taken before!

Directions:
1. Choose one of the unusual destinations listed on the tickets below. Pretend that you've just returned from a trip there.
2. Now pretend that you must give a speech to a travel club about your trip. You want your listeners to feel as if they're standing right in the place you visited. Fill in these blanks with some of your descriptions:

    What did you *see* there? _____

    What did you *hear* there? _____

    What did you *smell* there? _____

3. On a 6" x 6" piece of notebook paper, write a descriptive paragraph about your trip. Begin with a topic sentence that includes the name of the place you visited. Add three to five details from your lists above. End with a conclusion that restates your topic sentence.
4. Fold a 7" x 7" piece of construction paper in half.
5. Cut out the passport. Glue it to the front of your folded piece of construction paper.
6. Fill in the blanks on the passport. Draw and color a picture of yourself in the box.
7. Open your passport. Glue your paragraph inside.

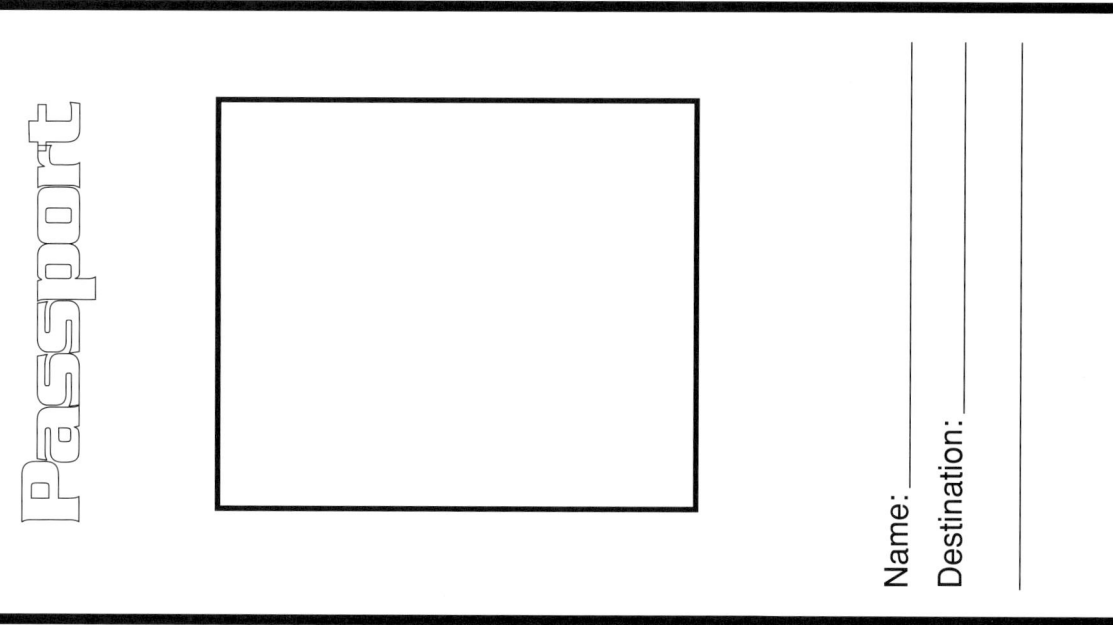

Passport

Name: _____

Destination: _____

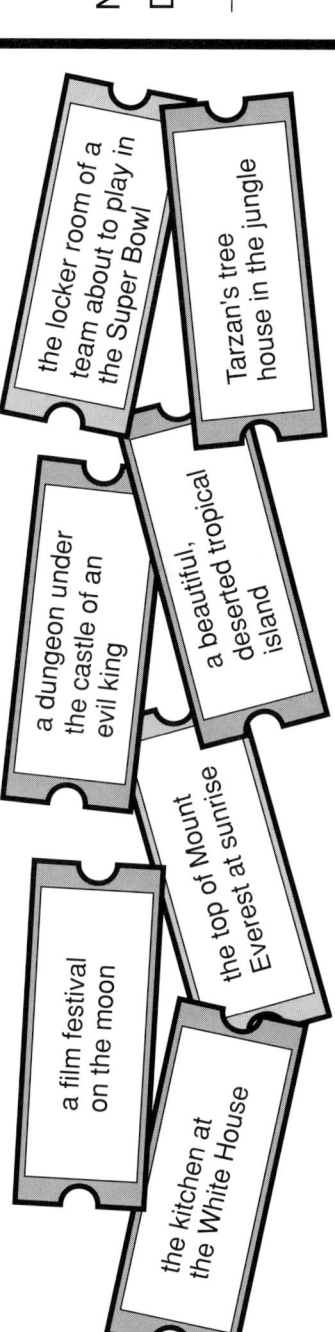

- the locker room of a team about to play in the Super Bowl
- Tarzan's tree house in the jungle
- a dungeon under the castle of an evil king
- a beautiful, deserted tropical island
- a film festival on the moon
- the top of Mount Everest at sunrise
- the kitchen at the White House

©2000 The Education Center, Inc. • *The Best Of The Mailbox® Writing • Intermediate* • TEC1485

Note To Teacher: Provide students with scissors, glue, crayons or markers, and construction paper. Display finished passports on a bulletin board titled "It's Just Like You Described It!"

Name _____   Paragraphs: writing narrative paragraphs

This Is Your Life!

Everyone's life has its interesting moments! Now's the time to share some of yours!

Directions:
1. Color and cut out the booklet cover below.
2. Glue it onto a piece of construction paper and trim the edges. Punch holes where indicated.
3. Trace the cover onto a piece of notebook paper; then cut out the tracing.
4. Choose one of the topic sentences listed below. On the piece of notebook paper, write a paragraph using the topic sentence. Be sure to give the events in the order in which they happened.
5. Use brads to attach your finished paragraph behind the cover.
6. If you like, add a page with an illustration of the paragraph.

Now build your booklet by writing other paragraphs on the topics listed below. How many pages can you add to your booklet?

Topic sentences

It was the funniest thing that ever happened to me.
It was the scariest thing that ever happened to me.
It was the most embarrassing thing that ever happened to me.
It was the most exciting thing that ever happened to me.
It was the most surprising thing that ever happened to me.
It was the most annoying thing that ever happened to me.
It was the saddest thing that ever happened to me.
It was the most wonderful thing that ever happened to me.

This Is Your Life,

_____ !
name

©2000 The Education Center, Inc. • *The Best Of* The Mailbox® *Writing* • *Intermediate* • TEC1485

CHANNEL   VOLUME   OFF/ON

Note To Teacher: Provide scissors, glue, construction paper, crayons or markers, a hole puncher, and brads. See "Writing Narrative Paragraphs" on page 33 for more information on using this activity.

Ready-To-Use Cards For Writing Paragraphs

Duplicate, laminate, and cut apart the cards on pages 41 and 42. Then duplicate the reproducibles below and on page 40 so that you will have a master copy of each. Use the cards with "Details, Details, Details" on page 31.

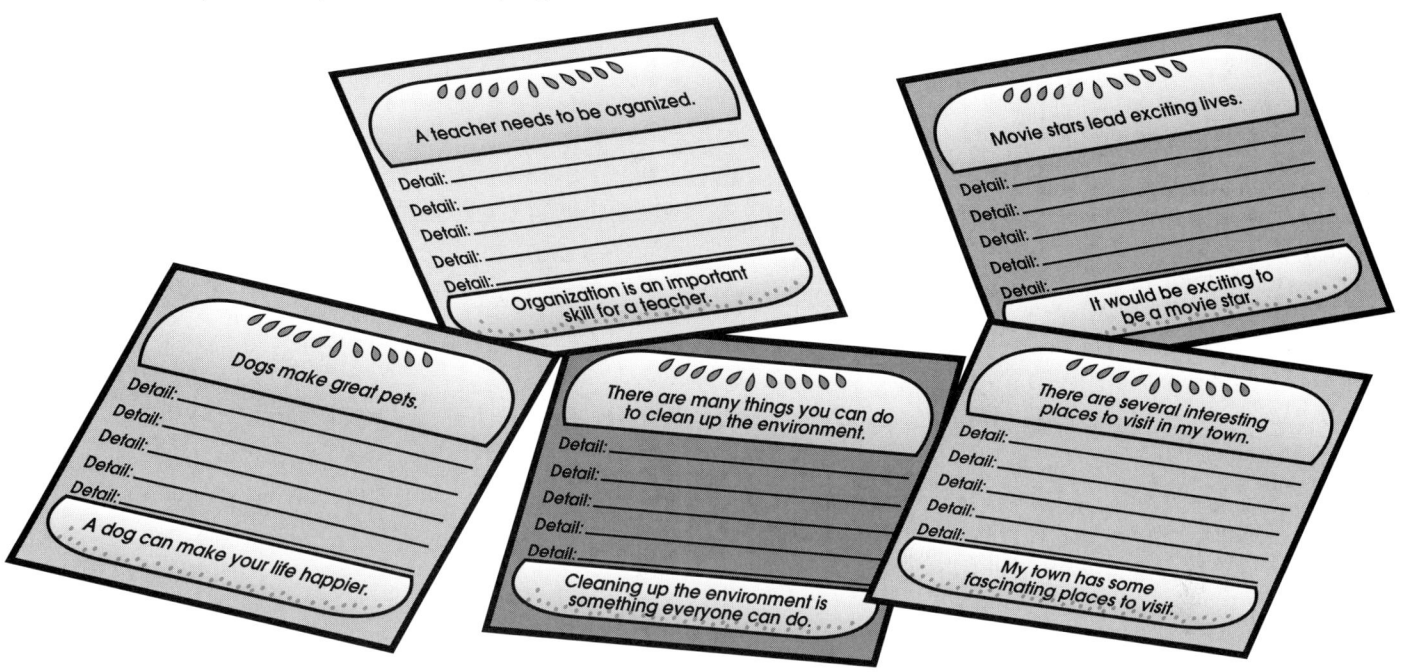

Use the "Digging Up A Good Idea" reproducible with the cards on pages 41 and 42.

Name _____

Digging Up A Good Idea

Need a paragraph starter? Try one of these! Each time you use one of the following topic sentences, write its number in a bone. How quickly can you fill in all of the bones?

1. I'll never forget the time that I _____.
2. A _____ makes the perfect pet.
3. If I could travel to any place in the world, I would go to _____.
4. If I had my choice, I'd rather be alone (or with my friends).
5. I have strong opinions about the clothes I wear.
6. My school has some very good things about it.
7. My school has some problems that should be worked on.
8. Being a police officer would be a great (or terrible) job.
9. I have a special place that I go to be alone.
10. Being a good friend is hard (or easy).
11. One career I am interested in is _____.
12. Recess is a fun time.
13. There are many places in my town to have a good time.
14. There are advantages to being the oldest (or youngest) child.
15. You can't always believe television commercials.
16. It would be interesting to spend an afternoon with _____.

Idea bank

©2000 The Education Center, Inc. • *The Best Of The Mailbox® Writing • Intermediate* • TEC1485

Name _____ Writing a paragraph: checklist

The Secret To Writing Gr-r-r-eat Paragraphs

You—yes, YOU—can write a great paragraph if you just follow the right steps in the right order. Use this form to write a paragraph on any topic.

1. What is your topic? _____

2. What will you say about your topic? (In other words, what are you trying to prove about the topic?) _____
_____
_____

Rewrite your answer in the form of a topic sentence:
_____
_____
_____

3. List several details that will support, explain, or prove what you want to say about your topic sentence.
   a. _____
   b. _____
   c. _____
   d. _____
   e. _____
   f. _____
   g. _____

4. Decide which details will do the best job of helping you say what you want to say about the topic. Which are the most interesting? Which tell the most important things about the topic? Which do the best job of proving, explaining, or supporting your topic sentence? Draw a circle around the letters of the details you will use in your paragraph.

5. What is your conclusion (the topic sentence rewritten)? _____
_____
_____

6. Now you're ready to write your paragraph on the back of this sheet or another piece of paper. Remember the "sandwich technique": Start your paragraph with your topic sentence. Fill in the middle with your details. End with your conclusion.

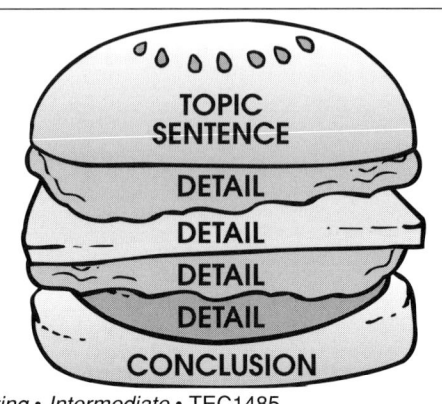

©2000 The Education Center, Inc. • *The Best Of The Mailbox® Writing • Intermediate* • TEC1485

Note To Teacher: Use with "Writing Topic Sentences" on page 32, and the cards on pages 41 and 42.

A teacher needs to be organized. Detail: _____ Detail: _____ Detail: _____ Detail: _____ Detail: _____ Organization is an important skill for a teacher.	The president of the United States has a hard job. Detail: _____ Detail: _____ Detail: _____ Detail: _____ Detail: _____ Being president would be a real challenge.
There are many things you can do to clean up the environment. Detail: _____ Detail: _____ Detail: _____ Detail: _____ Detail: _____ Cleaning up the environment is something everyone can do.	Movie stars lead exciting lives. Detail: _____ Detail: _____ Detail: _____ Detail: _____ Detail: _____ It would be exciting to be a movie star.
Dogs make great pets. Detail: _____ Detail: _____ Detail: _____ Detail: _____ Detail: _____ A dog can make your life happier.	There are several interesting places to visit in my town. Detail: _____ Detail: _____ Detail: _____ Detail: _____ Detail: _____ My town has some fascinating places to visit.
It would be great to be an only child. Detail: _____ Detail: _____ Detail: _____ Detail: _____ Detail: _____ Being an only child has advantages.	Playing football can be dangerous. Detail: _____ Detail: _____ Detail: _____ Detail: _____ Detail: _____ Football can be a dangerous sport.

It would be fun to have a twin.	Computers help people in many ways.
Detail: _____	Detail: _____
Detail: _____	Detail: _____
Detail: _____	Detail: _____
Detail: _____	Detail: _____
Detail: _____	Detail: _____
Being a twin would be terrific.	Computers are very useful.

Smoking is bad for your health.	The elephant is an unusual animal.
Detail: _____	Detail: _____
Detail: _____	Detail: _____
Detail: _____	Detail: _____
Detail: _____	Detail: _____
Detail: _____	Detail: _____
There are many reasons not to smoke.	Elephants are interesting in many ways.

People read books for different reasons.	There are several ways to drive your older sister crazy.
Detail: _____	Detail: _____
Detail: _____	Detail: _____
Detail: _____	Detail: _____
Detail: _____	Detail: _____
Detail: _____	Detail: _____
There are many different reasons for reading.	It is not hard to annoy your older sister.

A pet can be a lot of work.	Every kid should have a way to earn extra spending money.
Detail: _____	Detail: _____
Detail: _____	Detail: _____
Detail: _____	Detail: _____
Detail: _____	Detail: _____
Detail: _____	Detail: _____
Having a pet is a big responsibility.	Earning money is important for kids.

Cool Writing Activities For Cold Days

Brrr—December and January mean cooler weather and often-restless kids. Grab your students' attention and heat up their writing skills at the same time with these cool and creative projects. The weather outside my be frightful—but the enthusiasm inside will be delightful!

by Chris Christensen

To Help Mankind

Nobel Prizes are awarded each year on December 10 to people who are judged to have made the greatest contributions toward helping mankind. Though your students may not be famous peace activists or physicists, they can contribute to helping those around them. Emphasize this point by making Nobel Prize booklets. Duplicate the booklet cover on page 46 on yellow construction paper (one per student) and on white paper (four to six per student). After cutting out the pages, have students decorate their construction paper covers. On the white pages, have students complete the writing assignments given below. Bind finished booklets with colorful ribbon or yarn.

Booklet writing assignments:

A. Describe ways that you show your family and friends that you care for them.
B. Describe a situation that involves conflict. How could the problem be solved peacefully?
C. If you could contribute one thing for the good of mankind, what would it be? Explain your choice.

Christmas Candy

Eating candy in class? You bet! Give each student a piece of peppermint candy. While everyone enjoys the sweet treat, brainstorm a list of words and phrases describing the candy. After you've got a long list on the board, give each child a white paper plate.

On the back of the plate, have each student draw red lines to resemble peppermint candy. The child then writes the words "PEPPERMINT CANDY" vertically on the plate. He uses the letters and the list on the board to write words or phrases to describe the entire sensory experience of eating the candy—its taste, smell, appearance, etc. Have students glue their finished candies to green construction paper before displaying.

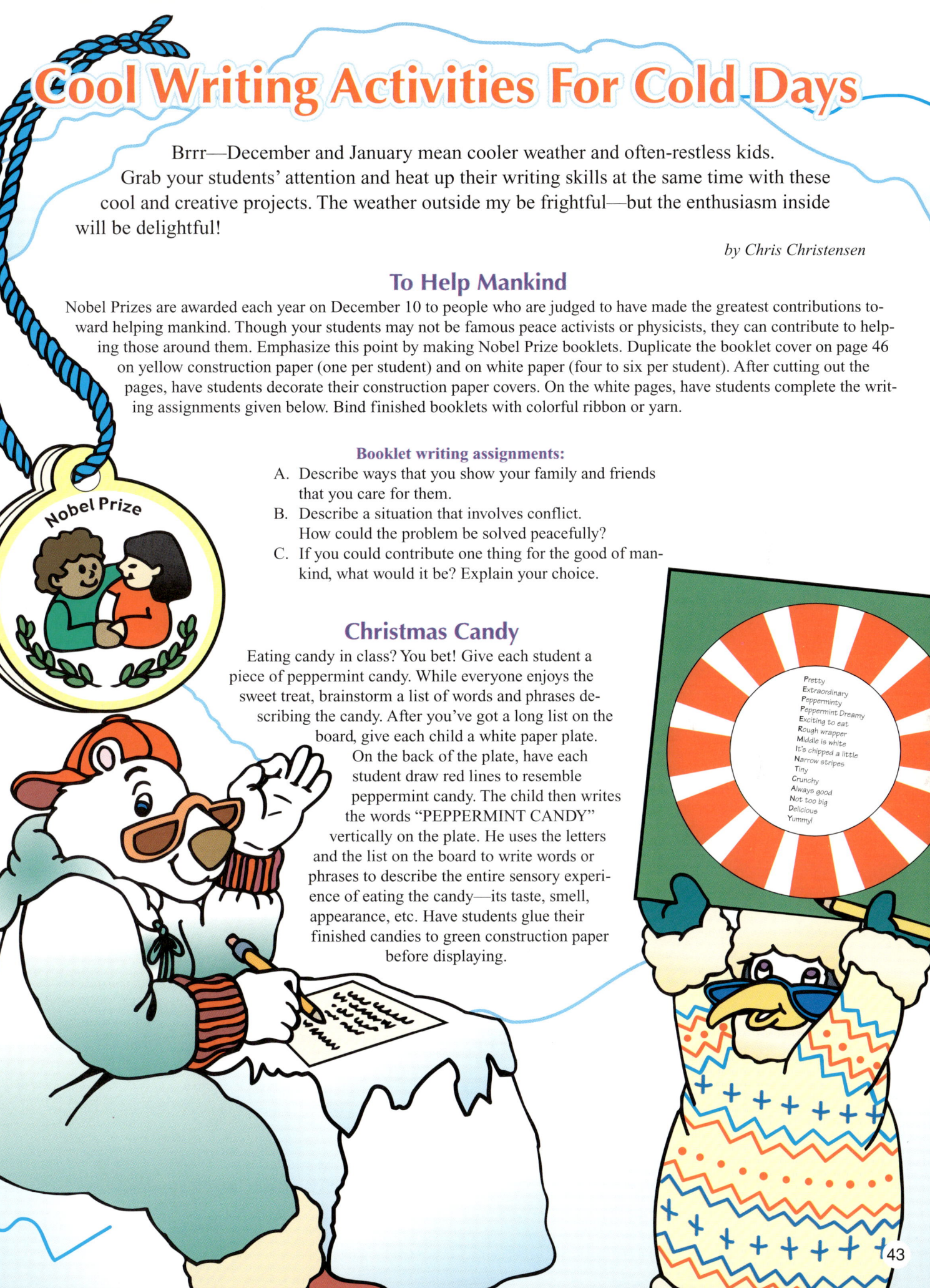

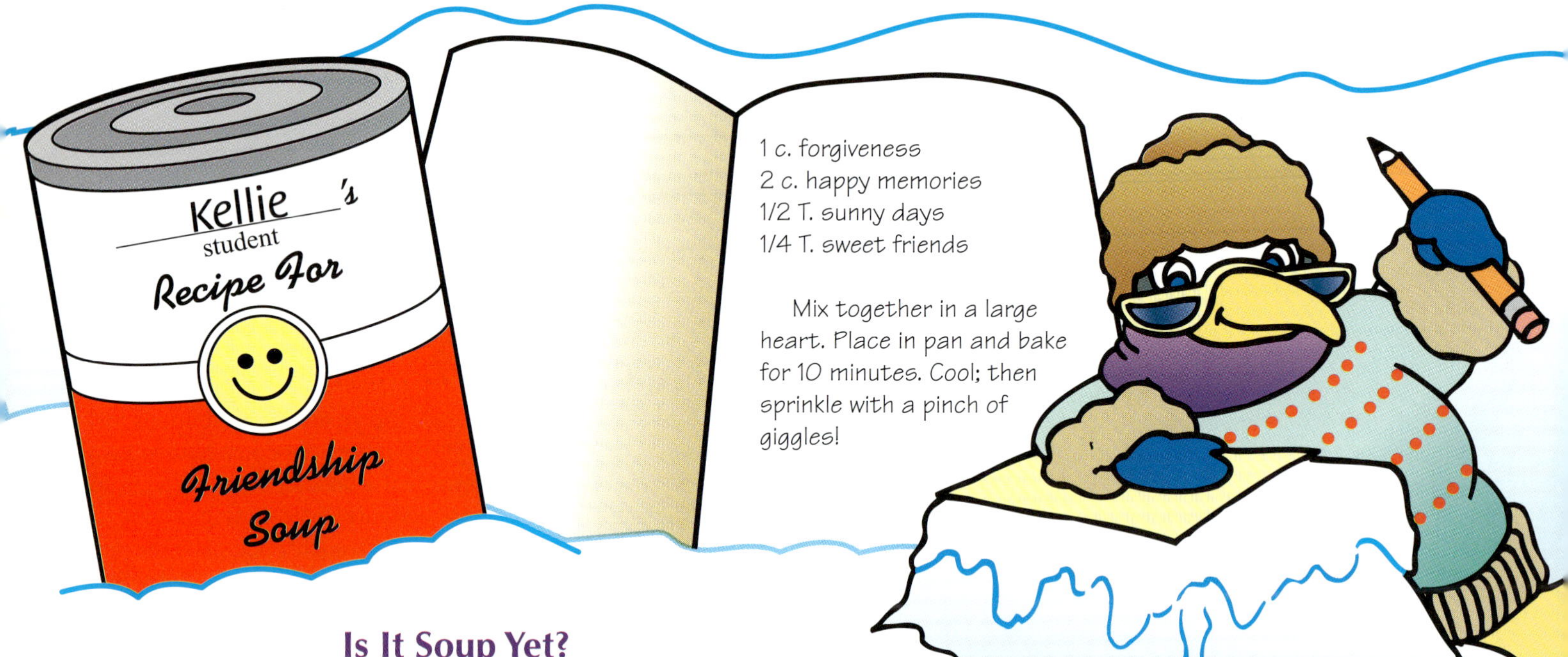

Kellie's student
Recipe For
Friendship Soup

1 c. forgiveness
2 c. happy memories
1/2 T. sunny days
1/4 T. sweet friends

Mix together in a large heart. Place in pan and bake for 10 minutes. Cool; then sprinkle with a pinch of giggles!

Is It Soup Yet?

What better month to celebrate National Soup Month than January? And what better concoction to cook up than a nice, steaming pot of Friendship Soup? Have students brainstorm a list of things that make people happy such as helpfulness, kindness, and doing a good job on a project. Duplicate the soup can pattern on page 46. Have each student glue his pattern on a folded piece of white paper, placing the left edge on the fold where indicated. The child then cuts out the can to make a folded card. Inside the card, have the student write his own recipe for friendship soup, using the list on the board to help him choose his ingredients. After coloring the covers, have students pin their cards to an "Is It Soup Yet?" bulletin board. Mmmmm—good!

National Nothing Day

Here it is—a day created to give Americans time to just sit without celebrating anything! On January 16, celebrate this unusual "non-holiday" by completing any of these fun-filled writing activities:
- List at least ten things you *could* do when you say, "There's nothing to do!"
- Research and write a paragraph about a topic you know nothing about.
- Describe a day when nothing went right.
- List five things you simply must do on National Nothing Day.
- Plan a special way your class could observe National Nothing Day.

Do You See Changes, Dr. King?

Dr. Martin Luther King lost his life in the service of peace and equality. If he were alive today, what would Dr. King see? After discussing Dr. King's work, ask students what changes have taken place in America and the world since his death. How would he feel about these changes? Would he think enough change has been accomplished? What situations would he think still need to be changed?

After discussing these questions, have each student pretend he is Dr. King and write a journal entry describing the positive changes he sees happening in the world today. Include plans Dr. King might have to improve situations that still need changing. Have students work as peer editors to proofread and edit each other's writings; then have each child copy his rewritten version onto a sheet of white construction paper that has been cut into a cloud shape. The student then glues the cloud at the top of a large piece of black paper. Next the student traces two handprints, one on brown paper and one on manila paper. The child cuts out the handprints, interlaces the fingers, and glues them to the bottom of the black paper. Post finished projects in a hallway for other classes to admire.

Name_____ Creative writing and thinking

Bah—HUMBUG!

Have you ever heard someone say, "HUMBUG"? This is an expression made famous in a story by Charles Dickens called *A Christmas Carol*. But what exactly is a humbug? Is it similar to a ladybug? A sow bug?

You can set the record straight! In the box below, draw a picture showing what *you* think a humbug looks like.

Answer the following questions in complete sentences. Use the back of this paper if you need more space.

1. Where do humbugs like to live? _____
   _____
   _____

2. What is the favorite food of humbugs? _____
   _____
   _____

3. Describe the sound humbugs make. Tell how the sound is made. _____
   _____
   _____

4. Describe how humbugs travel from place to place. _____
   _____
   _____

5. Describe any special markings or physical characteristics of humbugs. _____
   _____
   _____

6. How are humbugs useful to man? _____
   _____
   _____

Bonus Box: Name the character in *A Christmas Carol* who made the expression "humbug" famous.

©2000 The Education Center, Inc. • *The Best Of* The Mailbox® *Writing* • Intermediate • TEC1485

Patterns

For instructions on using this pattern, see "To Help Mankind" on page 43.

Punch a hole on the X and string with yarn or ribbon.

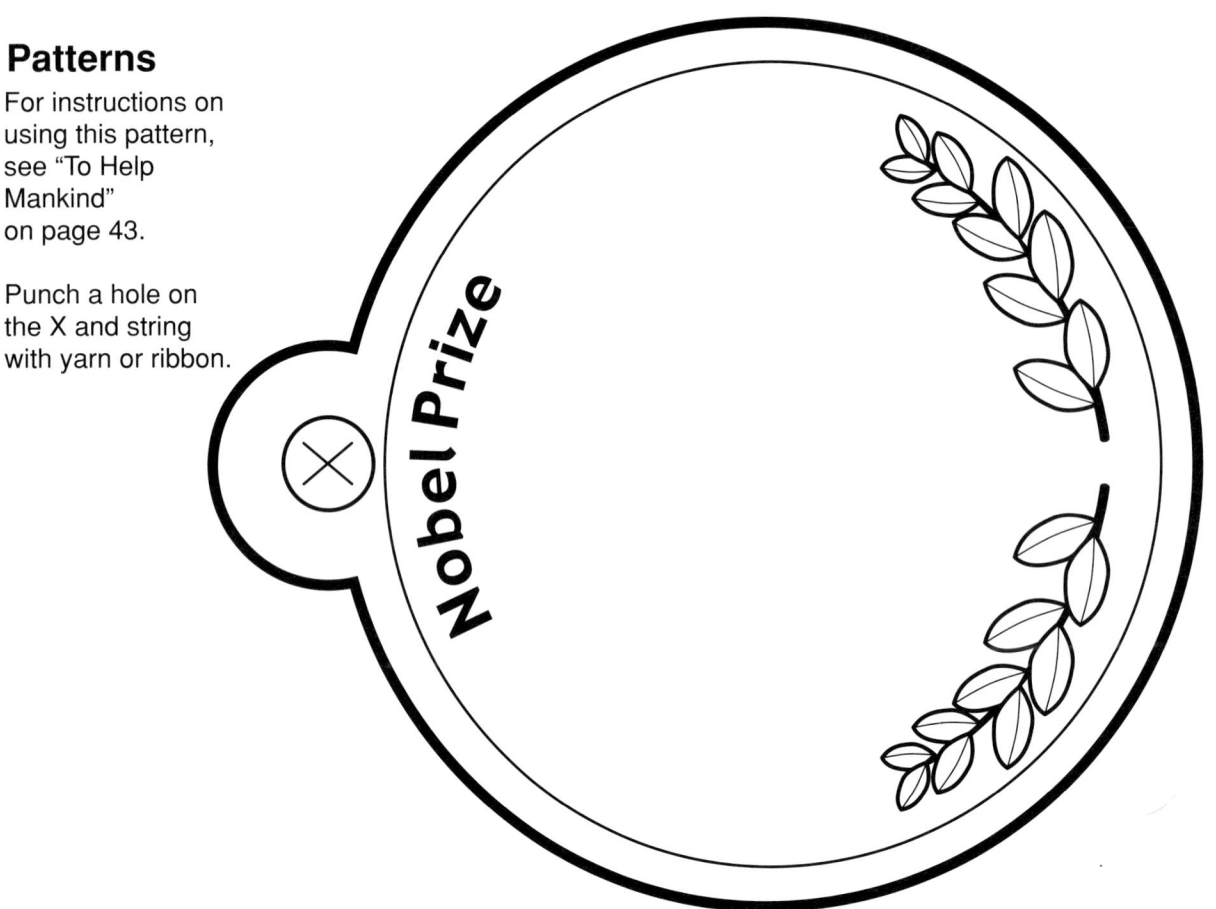

©2000 The Education Center, Inc. • *The Best Of* The Mailbox® *Writing* • *Intermediate* • TEC1485

For instructions on using this pattern, see "Is It Soup Yet?" on page 44.

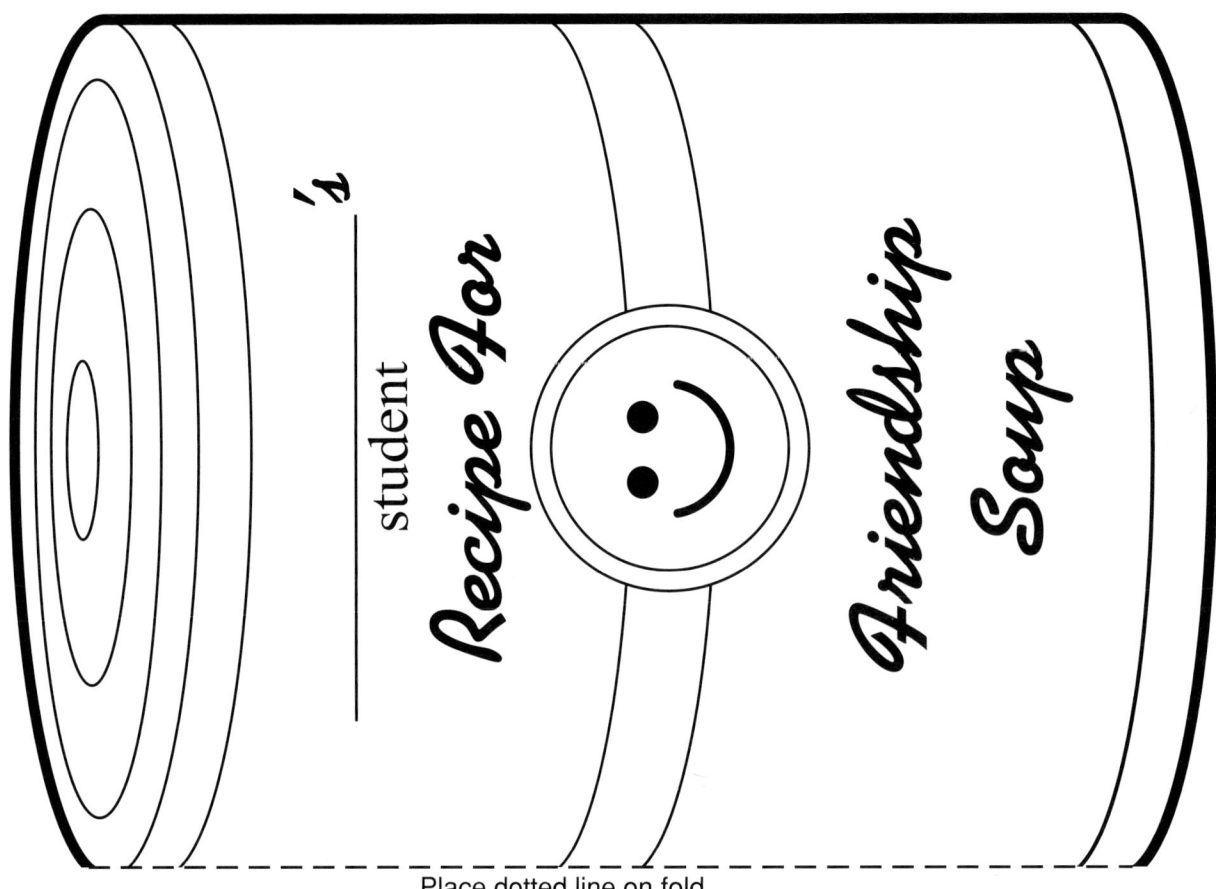

Place dotted line on fold.

©2000 The Education Center, Inc. • *The Best Of* The Mailbox® *Writing* • *Intermediate* • TEC1485

Journal Topics For Each Month

Looking for original and thought-provoking journal topics for students to write about? Look no further than the following topics created for each month of the school year. Use the reproducible journal covers on pages 71–76 to help students make their very own personal journals.

Tips For Using Journals And These Topics

- Duplicate a class supply of each month's pages. Have each student store his copies and journal in a pocket folder. During journal time, students can select the ideas that interest them.

- Duplicate each month's pages. At the beginning of the month, cut the individual ideas apart and place them in a basket. Each morning let a volunteer select the day's writing topic by drawing a slip from the basket.

- Cut apart the individual ideas and glue each to an index card. File the cards in a box by month; then place the box at a writing center. When a student gets stuck for a writing idea during writing workshop, let him browse through the ideas for that month.

- Model journal writing so that it doesn't become just another form of busywork. When students are writing in their journals, be sure to write in yours. Be ready to share your writings with students.

- No teacher has time to read all of her students' journals every day. To save time, purchase five colors of self-sticking dots. Put a dot on the outside cover of each journal. Read and respond to only one colored set of journals each day or week.

August Journal Suggestions

- Vacation has come to an end, and it's back-to-school time! What are you going to pack in your summer keepsake box?

- August is Foot Health Month. What does the idiom "He really put his foot in his mouth" mean? Write about a time when you put your foot in your mouth.

- August marks the beginning of the school year in many parts of the country. What do you think your teacher should know about you to help you have a successful school year?

- National Mustard Day is observed by condiment lovers on August 5. Are you more like plain mustard or the bold and spicy variety? Explain.

- Former astronaut Neil Armstrong, the first human to walk on the moon, was born on August 5, 1930. Do you have the "right stuff" to be an astronaut? Why or why not?

- August 6 marks Celebration Of Peace Fest in Japan. What can you do to promote peace in your school? Your home? Your neighborhood? The world?

- August 19 is President Bill Clinton's birthday. After he blows out the candles on his birthday cake, what would you like to sit down and chat with him about?

- August 22 is Be An Angel Day. Describe one angelic thing you could do for someone today. (Then do it!)

- Oscar-winning actress Marlee Matlin was born on August 24, 1965. Have you ever given an "award-winning" performance? Explain.

- On August 28, 1963, Dr. Martin Luther King, Jr., led the famous March on Washington to promote civil rights. What do you think still needs to be done to make equal rights a reality for everyone? How can you help?

- Scott Hamilton—an American skater who won a gold medal in the Olympics—was born on August 28, 1958. Describe how you would feel if you won an Olympic medal. What would you say to the world when you accepted your medal?

- The recognized authority on games, Edmond Hoyle, died on August 29, 1769. What are you qualified to be an authority on?

August Journal Suggestions

- Friendship Day is observed the first Sunday in August. What are the qualities of a good friend? In what ways are you a good friend?

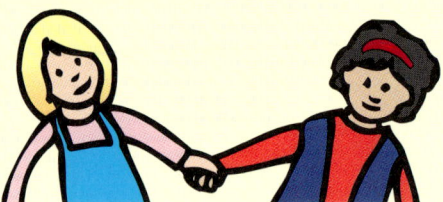

- International Clown Week is held the first full week in August. How do you think teachers feel when kids "clown around"? When is it appropriate to clown around? When is it inappropriate?

- On August 15, 1965, Frank Mitchell became the first Black American to serve as a page in the U.S. House of Representatives. What would you like to be the "first" to accomplish?

- National Aviation Week (the week that includes August 19) helps to increase awareness of aviation history. Which would you rather do: fly around the world on the Concorde jet or ride on the space shuttle? Explain your answer.

- On National Relaxation Day (August 15), people are supposed to totally relax. How do you relax? Describe a totally relaxing day.

- The first commercial advertisement was broadcast on a New York radio station on August 22, 1922. What do you think of the large payments celebrities receive to advertise products? Do you think these stars really use the products they sell? Should they?

- The U.S. *Voyager 2* spacecraft was launched in 1977. It had its first close encounter with the planet Neptune on August 24, 1989. Do you think there is life on other planets? Why or why not?

- On Kiss-and-Make-Up-Day (August 25), you can mend broken relationships. Could you forgive a friend who had betrayed you? Explain your answer.

- Women were given the right to vote on August 26, 1920, when the 19th Amendment was passed. Do you think the present voting age of 18 should be lowered? Explain your answer.

September Journal Suggestions

- September is National Chicken Month. Is there anything that you are "chicken" to do? Has anyone ever called you a chicken? How did the remark make you feel?

- September is National Courtesy Month. If someone is rude to you, how do you handle it?

- Since September is Self-Improvement Month, what would you most like to improve about yourself? Write a plan for achieving your goal.

- Cartoonist Cathy Lee Guisewite (creator and writer of "Cathy") celebrates her birthday on September 5. Which cartoon character are you most like? Explain.

- Be Late For Something Day is September 5. What's your best, most creative excuse for turning in homework late? Did it work?

- On September 8, 1921, the first Miss America was crowned. Do you think beauty pageants should still be held? Explain.

- California became the 31st state on September 9, 1850. Would the threat of a possible earthquake affect your feelings about living in California? Explain.

- Citizenship Day is September 17. In your opinion, what are the responsibilities of a good citizen?

- The birth of Chinese philosopher Confucius is observed on September 21. What's the wisest thing you have ever done?

- World Gratitude Day is September 21. For whom or what are you most grateful?

- It's football time again! From whose vantage point would you prefer to view a game: as a cheerleader on the sidelines, as a field-goal kicker, or as a reporter covering the game?

- On September 25, 1877, the first cream separator was patented. What do you think of separate schools for boys and girls? Would you like to attend such a school? Why or why not?

- National One-Hit Wonder Day (September 25) salutes rock-and-roll stars who had only one big hit song. What's the one thing for which you'd most like to be remembered?

September Journal Suggestions

- September is National Piano Month. How do you feel about parents making a child take music lessons?

- September is Cable TV Month. How would your family survive without television for a whole month?

- Library Card Sign-Up Month is observed in September. What are the qualities of a good book? What is the best book you've ever read? Why did you like this book so much?

- Labor Day is the first Monday in September. What should our country do about helping the unemployed people in America today?

- Emma M. Nutt Day honors the first female telephone operator, who began her career on September 1, 1878. What career would you like to pursue? How can you begin to prepare yourself now for this job?

- George Eastman patented the Kodak camera on September 4, 1888. You've been asked to take one photo that will tell the story of life in America today. What would you photograph? Why?

- Newspaper Carrier Day (September 4) honors ten-year-old Barney Flaherty, who answered a news carrier ad in 1833. Should kids under the age of 16 be allowed to hold part-time jobs? Why or why not?

- September 7 marks the birthday of a famous artist named Grandma Moses. She didn't start painting until she was 78 years old, proving that it's never too late! What do you want to begin before it's too late?

- Candy man Milton Hershey was born on September 13, 1847. If you could create a product that would bear your name, what would it be? Why would you create this product?

- Magician David Copperfield—famous for his fantastic illusions—was born on September 16, 1956. Have you ever been fooled by someone or something that really wasn't what he/she/it seemed?

- Mickey Mouse was introduced in a Disney cartoon on September 19, 1928. Are you more like Mickey Mouse or Donald Duck? Explain your answer.

- On September 20, 1973, tennis star Billie Jean King defeated Bobby Riggs in a "Battle of the Sexes" tennis match. Why do you think we haven't elected a female president yet?

- Dear Diary Day is celebrated on September 22. If you found a friend's diary, would you read it? Why or why not?

- The birthday of the ice-cream cone is celebrated on September 22. If someone described you by naming an ice-cream flavor, what flavor would he or she name? Explain your answer.

- The United States established a "regular army" of 700 men on September 29, 1789. Do you think every American should be required to serve in the military for a period of time? Should women be allowed to fight in combat zones? Explain your answers.

October Journal Suggestions

- October is National Clock Month. What are some things you like to do when you have a lot of extra time on your hands?

- October is Adopt-a-Shelter-Dog Month. What do you think is the best way to control overpopulation of dogs and cats in this country?

- The first week in October is Universal Children's Week. What is something that your family could do to celebrate this special week?

- October 2 marks the anniversary of the famous comic strip "PEANUTS," starring Charlie Brown and Snoopy. Who is your favorite comic strip character? Why does this character appeal to you?

- How long would it take *you* to get organized? Get Organized Week is celebrated the first full week in October. What are some things you could do to become better organized?

- National Newspaper Week is the first full week in October, while National Pet Peeve Week is celebrated the second full week in October. Write a letter to the editor of your local paper. Describe your pet peeve and what you'd like to see done about it.

- Eleanor Roosevelt, who was our country's first lady from 1933 to 1945, was born on October 11, 1884. Once her husband Franklin became president, Eleanor couldn't go anywhere without being recognized and surrounded by crowds of people. Would you like to be famous like the first lady? Why or why not?

- World Poetry Day is October 15. What are the characteristics of a "good" poem? When you read a poem that you really like, how does it make you feel?

- October 15 is National Grouch Day. List ten things that are sure to make your parents grouchy.

- October 16 is World Food Day. Many people who live in countries poorer than the United States do not have enough food to eat. Do you think Americans have a responsibility to help feed the people who live in these poor countries? Why or why not?

- National Business Women's Week is celebrated annually starting the third Monday in October. Think about a business woman that you know. What do you think makes this woman successful?

- October 18 is Alaska Day. Imagine yourself in Alaska on a winter day; then complete this sentence as humorously as you can: "It was so cold that…."

- Did you know that October 19 is Evaluate Your Life Day? List three things you would like to accomplish so that 20 years from now you'll be proud when you evaluate your life.

- The swallows always leave San Juan Capistrano, California, on October 23. They always return on March 19. What special place have you visited that you'd like to return to? Why is this place so special to you?

- Peace, Friendship and Good Will Week is the pleasant name of the last week in October. What would you like to tell important world leaders about how to observe this week?

October Journal Suggestions

- October is National Communicate With Your Kid Month. Its purpose is to promote better communication between teenagers and their parents. In your opinion, which is tougher: being a teenager or being the parent of a teenager? Explain.

- Family History Month is observed in October. Describe an event in the life of your family that you would definitely include in a book entitled *My Family History*.

- October is National Youth Against Tobacco Month. Write a letter to a friend (young person or adult) encouraging him or her to stop smoking.

- The first full week in October is Fire Prevention Week. What's something that really makes you "hot under the collar" (angry)?

- Cornelius Crane celebrates his birthday on October 8. You know him better as actor/comedian Chevy Chase. Why do you think so many entertainers change their names? If you could change your name, what would you change it to? Why?

- Martin Luther King, Jr., received the Nobel Peace Prize on October 14, 1964. If you could work for peace between two people, two groups of people, or two nations, who would they be? Explain.

- Dictionary Day (October 16) honors the birthday of Noah Webster. If you could put in a good word about yourself to your teacher, what would you say?

- October 23 is Michael Crichton's birthday. Crichton wrote the book *Jurassic Park*, on which the popular movie was based. What do you think of the idea of re-creating creatures of long ago, such as dinosaurs?

- October 24 is the birth anniversary of Belva A. Lockwood. In 1884 she became the first woman formally nominated to be president of the United States. Do you think the United States will soon have a woman president? Why or why not?

- The Mount Rushmore National Memorial was completed on October 31, 1941. Suppose one more face were added to this monument. Who do you think deserves such an honor? Why?

November Journal Suggestions

- November is Aviation History Month. Which do you think is the more important invention: the automobile or the airplane? Explain the reasons for your choice.

- Project Red Ribbon (November 1–January 1) is a national effort to encourage Americans not to drink and drive. Each participant attaches a red ribbon to his vehicle as a sign that he is committed to this effort. Write about why you support Project Red Ribbon. Copy your paragraph on an index card and attach a red ribbon to it. Give the card to someone who drives.

- November 6 marks the birth anniversary of Adolphe Sax. He was a Belgian musician who invented—you guessed it!—the saxophone. Which would you rather be: a world-renowned pianist, a drummer in a rock-and-roll band, or a jazz saxophonist? Explain.

- The first week in November marks the halfway point of autumn. If you could choose one of the four seasons to last all year long, which would you choose? Why?

- On November 8, 1895, German physicist Wilhelm C. Roentgen discovered X rays. He called them X rays because he didn't understand what they were at first! Now, over 100 years later, what great scientific discovery would you wish for? Why?

- The song "God Bless America" was first performed on radio on November 11, 1938. Some people think "God Bless America" would be a better national anthem for our country than "The Star-Spangled Banner." What do you think?

- November celebrates American Education Week. Describe one important life lesson that you learned from a past teacher. Why do you remember this lesson so well?

- Robert Fulton, inventor of the steamboat, was born November 14, 1765. Some people called his ship "Fulton's Folly" because they thought it would never work. Describe a new invention that would have amazed people of the 19th century.

- National Farm-City Week is celebrated during the week of Thanksgiving. Would you rather live on a farm or in a large city? Give several reasons for your choice.

- Mickey Mouse first appeared November 18, 1928, on the screen of the Colony Theatre in New York City. This Walt Disney film, *Steamboat Willie*, was the first animated cartoon talking picture. Why do you think Mickey Mouse has remained popular for so many years?

- National Game And Puzzle Week (the last week in November) has two purposes: to increase appreciation of games and puzzles, and to promote spending time with family and friends. What game do you and your family (or you and your friends) enjoy playing together? Why is it so much fun?

- On November 26, 1789, President George Washington proclaimed the first U.S. holiday: Thanksgiving Day. It was a day for our entire nation to give thanks. What do you think our nation should be thankful for today?

- Madeleine L'Engle, author of *A Wrinkle In Time*, celebrates her birthday on November 29. Do you like science fiction books and movies? What's your favorite science fiction book (or movie)? Why?

November Journal Suggestions

- November is International Drum Month. Drumming truly is international. Why do you think drums are important in the music of so many different cultures?

- World Communication Week is observed the first week of November. If you could communicate with someone who speaks a different language, who would it be and what would you say?

- If you could interview your favorite author on November 1, National Authors' Day, what questions would you ask?

- Daniel Boone, one of our country's most famous frontiersmen and explorers, was born on November 2, 1734. Boone had a great deal of curiosity—that's what made him a great explorer. When is it a good thing to be curious? When can curiosity cause trouble?

- Sandwich Day is celebrated on November 3. What ingredients do you think would be needed to make "A Successful Student Sandwich"?

- James Naismith, the inventor of basketball, was born on November 6, 1861. Do you think that professional basketball players and other famous athletes should be careful about their behavior, since so many kids look up to them as role models? Or should they be able to live their lives without worrying about how their actions might influence other people? Give your opinion.

- November 11 marks the anniversary of the entombment of the Unknown Soldier of World War I in Arlington National Cemetery. What do you think is the best way to honor our veterans?

- On November 14, 1889, a reporter named Nellie Bly set off on a trip that took her around the world in a little over 72 days. Pretend that you have the chance to take a similar trip during summer vacation. Think about what you'd miss by being gone for over two months; think also about what you would gain by taking the trip. Would you be willing to take the trip? Why or why not?

- National Community Education Day is celebrated in November. This day promotes building relationships between schools and communities. Do you think communities should be involved in schools? Why or why not?

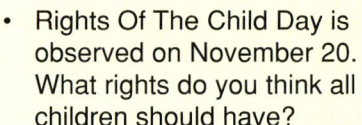

- For people who hate to hear "Have a nice day," there's Have A Bad Day Day on November 19. List ten friendly phrases you could use instead of "Have a nice day."

- Rights Of The Child Day is observed on November 20. What rights do you think all children should have?

- November 22 is National Stop The Violence Day. What would you say to someone who said, "Video games are too violent and are contributing to the increase in violence in our country"?

- Thanksgiving Day is celebrated on the fourth Thursday in November. What are some things you are thankful *didn't* happen this year?

January Journal Suggestions

- On January 1, 1892, Ellis Island was opened and began operation as a processing center for millions of immigrants. How do you think that our government should treat the millions of foreign refugees who are still trying to immigrate to the United States?

- In January, newly elected congressmen and congresswomen will take office. How do you feel about enacting term limits for elected officials?

- January 4 is the birthday of Louis Braille, who invented a special alphabet for blind people. What idea do you have that will make things easier for others?

- Trivia Day is observed on January 4. What fact that is important to you might seem like trivia to someone else?

- Jacob Grimm, the famous coauthor of *Grimm's Fairy Tales*, was born on January 4, 1785. Would you rather read fiction or nonfiction? Why?

- If you could share a peanut butter sandwich with George Washington Carver—the scientist who developed many by-products of peanuts and died on January 5, 1943—what would you talk about?

- Singer Elvis Presley was born on January 8, 1935. What are the disadvantages of being as famous as Elvis?

- On January 8, 1964, President Lyndon B. Johnson declared a War on Poverty in his State of the Union message. He stressed that improved education is one of the main ways to prevent poverty. How will your education help you become a successful adult?

- The third Monday in January is National Clean-Off-Your-Desk Day. In celebration, clean out your desk; then make a list of goals that you would like to accomplish in the new year.

- Born on January 11, 1842, philosopher and psychologist William James once wrote, "There is no worse lie than a truth misunderstood by those who hear it." What do you think James meant by this statement?

- Edwin "Buzz" Aldrin, former astronaut and one of the first three men on the moon, was born on January 20, 1930. In your opinion, should the United States continue to send astronauts to explore space? Explain your answer.

- John Hancock, the first signer of the Declaration of Independence, was born on January 23, 1737. How do you think your life would have been different if America was still a colony of England?

- National Handwriting Day is observed on January 23. From whom would you most like to receive a handwritten letter? Why?

- January 28 marks the anniversary of the explosion of the space shuttle *Challenger*. Most people agree that the astronauts who died in that accident were all heroes. In your opinion, what makes someone a hero?

- The Super Bowl football game is played annually in January. What are the advantages to being part of a team?

January Journal Suggestions

- On January 1, 1924, Frank Buckley Cooney of Minnesota invented the first "ink paste," or crayon. Which color best describes you? Explain.

- Each January, newspapers and magazines review the top news stories of the previous year. In your opinion, what were the top five news events of last year?

- January 1999 was year number ten in the Decade Of The Brain. Use your brain to figure out the best way to stick to your New Year's resolutions. Explain your plan—then stick to it!

- January is Diet Month. How could you help an overweight friend feel good about him- or herself?

- American seamstress Betsy Ross, who is often credited with sewing the first American flag, was born in Philadelphia on January 1, 1752. In your opinion, is the design of the American flag still a good one? Why? How would you redesign it?

- Martin Luther King's birthday is observed on Monday, January 15. In your opinion, what can students in your school do to improve relationships between people of different races?

- Answer Your Cat's Question Day is observed on January 22. If your pet could talk, what do you think it would say to you?

- Gold was discovered in California on January 24, 1848. The secret of this discovery leaked out to the public and the gold rush began. Have you ever told a secret? What were the consequences of telling it?

- Mark Goodson—creator of popular television game shows like "The Price Is Right"—was born on January 24, 1915. Why do you think game shows are so popular?

- The first nationally televised presidential news conference was held on January 25, 1961. In an election year, what questions would you most like to ask the major presidential candidates?

- Wolfgang Amadeus Mozart was born on January 27, 1756. He began performing at age three and composing at age five. What sacrifices do you think a prodigy (an extremely talented child or youth) would have to make in order to be successful? Do you think it would be worth it? Explain.

- On January 31, 1919, Jackie Robinson was born. He was the first black major-league baseball player. Would you rather be a "first," or follow in someone else's footsteps? Explain.

- Many people vacation in January after the holidays. What souvenir would you design for tourists to take home as a reminder of their visit to your town? Why?

February Journal Suggestions

- February is American Heart Month. What do you wish for most, from the bottom of your heart?

- February 1, Robinson Crusoe Day, is the anniversary of the 1709 rescue of Scottish sailor Alexander Selkirk. His adventures formed the basis for Daniel Defoe's famous book, *Robinson Crusoe*. If you were stranded on a remote island, what three things would you miss most about your life back home?

- Be An Encourager® Day is observed annually on February 1. Who has given YOU the most encouragement in your life so far? Explain your answer.

- On February 2, 1936, Babe Ruth was voted into the Baseball Hall of Fame in Cooperstown, New York. Who would you include in your personal Hall of Fame? Explain each choice.

- On February 3, 1690, the first American paper money was printed in Massachusetts. If you had to name ten things that money can't buy, what would you list? Write your list in the order of importance to you, with number one being the most important item.

- On February 4, 1861, the Confederate States of America was organized in Montgomery, Alabama. How might your life be different if the South had won the Civil War?

- February means the cold and flu season is upon us. What's the quickest way to help you feel better when you are sick? What's the quickest way to make you feel worse?

- During summer hot spells, merchants often advertise cool drinks and other items to remind you of the frosty, blizzardy days of winter. What could you invent that would get everyone in the mood for a midwinter heat wave? Explain your invention. Include a labeled drawing if you like.

- One of America's first weather forecasters, John Jeffries, was born on February 5, 1744. What weather term best describes how you feel today: sunny, stormy, cloudy, misty, foggy, breezy, or partly cloudy? Explain your answer.

- On February 12, 1870, women in the Territory of Utah were given the right to vote. In your opinion, what should be the legal voting age in this country? Give reasons for your opinion.

- On February 13, 1635, America's first public school—the Boston Latin School—was established. Do you think a college degree is a necessity these days? Give reasons for your answer.

- February is the birth month of "Honest Abe" Lincoln and George "I-cannot-tell-a-lie" Washington. If your best friend asked you an embarrassing question, would you tell the truth even if it was unpleasant or difficult to do so? Why or why not?

- Presidents' Day is observed on the third Monday of this month. In today's political campaigns, candidates often say unkind things about their opponents. They are also often criticized and watched closely by the media. Do you think that running for public office is worth going through these types of hassles? Explain your answer.

- On February 23, 1633, Samuel Pepys—author of a world-famous diary—was born in Cambridge, England. How would you feel if someone read your diary? What famous person's diary would you REALLY like to sneak a peek at?

February Journal Suggestions

- February is Black History Month, a time to spotlight the achievements of Black Americans. If you were to write the biography of a famous Black American, whom would you choose? What quality or accomplishment of this person do you most admire?

- February is National Children's Dental Health Month. What event always makes a big smile appear on your face whenever you happen to think of it?

- February 2 is Groundhog Day. An old belief says that if the groundhog sees his shadow when he emerges on this day, six more weeks of winter will follow. What do you like most—and least—about winter?

- The first American paper money was issued by Massachusetts on February 3, 1690. Should kids your age be rewarded with money for getting good grades? Explain your answer.

- Rosa Lee Parks, a civil rights leader, was born on February 4, 1913. Would you be willing to go to jail for protesting something that you thought was wrong? Explain your answer.

- American aviator Charles A. Lindbergh was born on February 4, 1902. He's known for his nonstop, solo flight across the Atlantic Ocean from New York to Paris in 1927. What's the bravest thing you've ever done solo?

- Baseball heroes Hank Aaron (born February 5, 1934) and Babe Ruth (born February 6, 1895) both set home-run records. Who do you think should be paid more: a teacher or a professional baseball player? Explain your answer.

- Laura Ingalls Wilder, famous for her Little House books, was born on February 7, 1867. If you could live in another period of American history, which one would you choose? Why?

- On February 8, 1910, the Boy Scouts of America were founded. What good deed could you perform that would make your sister/brother/parents a lot happier? What are the chances that you'll do it?

- Inventor Thomas A. Edison was born on February 11, 1847. During his lifetime he held more than 1,200 patents on items that have greatly affected our lives. What new invention does the world need most right now?

- Valentine's Day is celebrated on February 14. Whom would you most like to have a heart-to-heart talk with? Why?

- February 14 is Read To Your Child Day. If you could choose only one book to share with a younger child, what would it be? Why?

- On February 18, 1930, astronomer Clyde Tombaugh discovered the planet Pluto while watching the sky from an Arizona observatory. Do you think there is life as we know it in outer space? Why or why not?

- On February 21, 1866, Lucy Hobbs became the first woman to graduate from a dental school. What household chore/homework subject is "harder than pulling teeth" to get you to complete?

March Journal Suggestions

- March is National Women's History Month. Who do you think is the most influential woman in America today? Why did you choose this person?

- National Noodle Month is celebrated each year in March. "Use your noodle" and decide on one thing you can do to help your classroom run more smoothly.

- March is Peanut Butter Lover's Month. Which teacher at your school would you like to share a peanut-butter sandwich lunch with?

- The first full week in March is National Drug and Alcohol Awareness Week. How could you help a friend who has a drug or alcohol problem?

- On March 1, 1961, President John F. Kennedy began the Peace Corps. Would you commit two years of your life to serving in a foreign country as a Peace Corps volunteer? Why? Which country would you like to go to? How could you help this country?

- On March 3, 1847, Alexander Graham Bell—inventor of the telephone—was born. Should kids have their own personal phones? Why or why not?

- *Frankenstein*, written by Mary W. Shelley, was first published on March 11, 1818. Do you like scary books, movies, and television shows? Why or why not?

- The United States Military Academy at West Point, New York, was established on March 16, 1802. Do you think that women should be allowed to attend military schools? Do you think women should take part in military combat? Explain your answers.

- On March 17, we wear a bit of the green to celebrate St. Patrick's Day. Suppose you caught a leprechaun, and he led you to a pot of gold. What would you do with the gold?

- The mission at San Juan Capistrano, California, is known for the swallows that leave there every year in October to winter in the South. When the swallows return on March 19, people say it's spring. How do you know when it's spring?

- Escape artist Harry Houdini was born on March 24, 1874. From what task would you most like to escape?

- March 26 is Make Up Your Own Holiday Day. It's a special day that you may name for whatever you wish! Describe the holiday that you will create.

- On March 30, 1858, Hyman L. Lipman of Philadelphia patented a pencil with an attached eraser. What mistake have you made that you would like to erase?

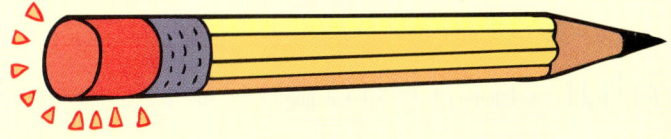

- People laughed at Secretary of State William H. Seward when he helped the United States buy Alaska from Russia on March 30, 1867. They thought he was foolish and called Alaska "Seward's Folly." Have you ever done anything that others thought was foolish? Were they right? Explain your answers.

- The Eiffel Tower was completed on March 31, 1889. This Paris tourist attraction is famous all over the world. Which would you most like to visit: the Eiffel Tower, the Leaning Tower of Pisa in Italy, Big Ben in London, or the Empire State Building in New York? Explain your answer.

March Journal Suggestions

- National Pig Day is March 1. If you could go to any restaurant and "pig out" for free, what restaurant would you visit? What exactly makes this restaurant so "pig-errific"?

- March is Youth Art Month. Would you rather be recognized for outstanding artistic, writing, or athletic ability? Explain your answer.

- Movie director Ron Howard was born on March 1, 1954. He started his career in show business as a child playing Opie on "The Andy Griffith Show." Would you like to be on a national television show? Give reasons for your answer.

- Dr. Seuss—whose real name was Theodor Geisel—was born March 2, 1904. His first book, *And To Think That I Saw It On Mulberry Street*, was rejected by 27 publishers before finally selling. Dr. Seuss succeeded because he was persistent! Write about a time when you were persistent and it paid off.

- March is National Frozen Food Month. Have you ever been "frozen" with fear? Describe what caused your fright and how you dealt with it.

- March 1–7 is Return The Borrowed Books Week. Do you agree with the old saying, "Neither a borrower nor a lender be"? Explain.

- Samuel Colt, inventor of the first pistol with a revolving cylinder, incorporated his Patent Arms Manufacturing Company on March 5, 1836. How do you feel about gun control?

- National Save Your Vision Week is observed the first full week in March. What do you see more clearly now than you used to see?

- When he played for the Philadelphia Warriors, basketball star Wilt Chamberlain scored 32 points in a game against Detroit on March 10, 1961. This made him the first basketball player to score more than 3,000 points in a season. How would you feel if you held a world record like Wilt Chamberlain? How would you feel if someone else broke your record?

- TV Turn-Off Week is observed annually the second week in March. Why do you think people watch so much television these days?

- On March 13, 1877, Chester Greenwood received a patent for his invention called "earmufflers." What sounds would you like your earmuffs to drown out?

- Albert Einstein—who was born March 14, 1879—once said, "Imagination is more important than knowledge." Do you agree or disagree? Explain your answer.

- Pocahontas (Rebecca Rolfe) died March 21, 1617. How do you think she would feel about the cartoon movie made about her? Explain.

- Composer Stephen Sondheim was born March 22, 1930. Annually his birthday is declared National Sing-Out Day. In your opinion, what's the best song ever written? Why is it your favorite?

- Liberty Day is March 23. It marks the anniversary of Patrick Henry's famous "give me liberty or give me death" speech. Exactly what liberties are kids your age entitled to these days? Why do you think these freedoms are important?

April Journal Suggestions

- April is Mathematics Education Month. Describe how you would find the sum of all the numbers from 1 to 100. When German mathematician Johann Gauss (born April 30, 1777) was ten years old, his teacher gave his class this problem to solve. Johann solved it quickly—and correctly!
  Hint: 1 + 100 = 101; 2 + 99 = 101; 3 + 98 = 101…

- April is Prevention Of Animal Cruelty Month. How do you feel when you see a wild animal that's been hit and killed on a highway? What about a cat or a dog? Explain.

- April Fools' Day is celebrated on April 1. What's the difference between a harmless prank and a harmful one? Describe a time when someone played a harmful prank on you. How did you feel?

- Helen Keller was blind and deaf. On April 5, 1887, her teacher (Anne Sullivan) held Helen's hand under running water and used her fingers to spell "water." At last, Helen made the connection that what her teacher was spelling was the word for water. If you had to give up your sight or hearing for one year, which would you give up? Why?

- April 7 is World Health Day. Write one thing you could do to become a healthier person. Then write a plan for how you can accomplish it.

- April 10 is the 100th day of this year. Complete the following topic sentence: "If I had a hundred…." Then add several more sentences explaining the reasons for your choice.

- Franklin D. Roosevelt died on April 12, 1945. He was the only president to serve more than two terms. In fact, he was elected to four consecutive terms! Today presidents are only allowed to serve two terms. Is this a good idea? Explain.

- On April 13, 1796, Jacob Crowninshield brought the first elephant to America. Imagine the surprise of many Americans who had never seen such an animal! Describe a time when you saw a particular animal for the very first time. Were you amazed? Frightened?

- Leonardo da Vinci—born on April 15, 1452—is known for two of the most famous pieces of art ever created: the *Last Supper* and the *Mona Lisa*. Why do you think the Mona Lisa has such a mysterious smile?

She smiles like that because she'd look silly like this. -Kevin

- The third week in April is National Coin Week. Some people have suggested that we should stop using pennies altogether—they're just not worth the bother. What do you think?

- Earth Day is celebrated annually on April 22. The theme of the first Earth Day in 1970 was "Give Earth A Chance." What does this theme mean to you today?

- April is National Humor Month. What's the funniest book you have ever read? What was so funny about it?

- Arbor Day, celebrated on the last Friday in April, reminds us of the importance of trees to our way of life. Look around you. Describe how trees are important in your life.

April Journal Suggestions

- April is the month known for its spring showers. For this reason, people often say it's "raining cats and dogs." What do you wish would pour down from the skies?

- A former slave named Robert became a very famous American hermit. He died on April 1, 1832, at his hermitage in Seekonk, Massachusetts. What do you think would be the advantages and disadvantages of a solitary life? Do you ever feel like becoming a hermit? Explain.

- April 2 is International Children's Book Day. It marks the birthday of Hans Christian Andersen. If you could trade places with a famous book character, whom would you select and why?

- Walter Hunt received a patent for inventing the safety pin on April 10, 1849. "Pin" your thinking cap on and explain four new uses for the safety pin.

- The ill-fated *Apollo 13* spacecraft was launched on April 11, 1970. After experiencing a problem with a ruptured oxygen tank, this flight's planned moon landing was cancelled. The crew successfully splashed down on April 17, 1970. Describe the qualities you think a person with a life-threatening job should possess.

- In addition to being an inventor and U.S. president, Thomas Jefferson—whose birthday was April 13, 1743—was also an architect. Architects design buildings. What features would you include in your design of an ideal school, home, or room?

- National Stress Awareness Day is observed annually in April. What things are stressful for you? Describe several different ways you could handle these pressure-causing incidents.

- Look-Alike Day (April 16) recognizes people who look like famous people. What famous person do you think you resemble? Does this make you happy? Explain. Would you like to trade places with this person? Why or why not?

- On April 24, 1800, the Library of Congress was established. Sir Richard Steele once said, "Reading is to the mind what exercise is to the body." What type of literature do you most often use to exercise your mind? Elaborate on the types of books you almost always choose to read.

- The annual Take Our Daughters To Work Day is recognized on the fourth Thursday in April. What occupation do you foresee yourself performing when you take your daughter to work in a few years? Explain.

- Gideon Sundback patented the zipper on April 29, 1913. Can you keep your lips zipped when someone confides in you, or do you always manage to spill the beans? Explain.

May Journal Suggestions

- Cartoon Art Appreciation Week is in May. What is your favorite cartoon? Why? If you could make one change in this cartoon, what would it be?

- In Korea, May 5 is Children's Day. A national holiday, Children's Day is a time when parents take their children on trips to amusement parks. How would you want to celebrate Children's Day?

- If we all gave up wearing socks for one day, there would be less laundry—which would help the environment! Now you know everything there is to know about No Socks Day (May 8). Title a paragraph "No _____ Day." Describe your new holiday, giving reasons why you think it is needed.

- Belle Boyd—born May 9, 1843—was a Confederate spy during the Civil War. Have you ever spied on someone? Has anyone ever spied on you? How did you feel?

- The first Tuesday of the first full week in May is National Teacher Day. If your teacher were chosen "Teacher of the Year" and you were asked to speak at a ceremony honoring him or her, what would you say?

- Irving Berlin, who wrote "God Bless America," was born on May 11, 1888. Although Berlin couldn't read or write music, he became one of America's best-known songwriters. He also lived to be 101 years old! If you live to be 100, what do you think life will be like in your old age?

- Edward Lear, the English poet known for his limericks, was born on May 12, 1812. Here's one of his limericks:
    There was an old man with a beard,
        Who said, "It is just as I feared—
            Two owls and a hen,
            Four larks and a wren
    Have all built their nests in my beard."
Write a silly limerick of your own. Use Lear's example as a guide to help you.

- Steveland Morris Hardaway—known as Stevie Wonder—was born on May 13, 1951. In 1986, Stevie and some friends recorded the song "That's What Friends Are For." Complete this topic sentence: "Friends are for…." Then add more sentences for a complete paragraph.

- The week including May 15 is National Police Week. What are some things you can do to make sure you're safe in your home as well as at school?

- Lyman Frank Baum—who was born May 15, 1856—wrote more than a dozen children's books about an enchanted land called Oz. Why do you think *The Wonderful Wizard Of Oz* became the most famous of all of Baum's books?

- On May 22, 1992, Johnny Carson hosted his last "Tonight" show. He had been a host of the show for nearly 30 years! If you had your very own talk show, what three people would you first invite to be your guests and what would you talk about?

- Dr. Sally Ride—the first American woman in space—was born on May 26, 1951. If you could accomplish a "first," what would it be? Why?

- The Dionne sisters—the first surviving quintuplets (five children born at a single birth)—were born on May 28, 1934, in Canada. How would you like to have four brothers and/or sisters, all the same age as you? How would your household change?

- Memorial Day is observed each year on the last Monday in May. On Memorial Day we remember those who have died, especially those who have died in wars. Should we have "sad" holidays such as Memorial Day? Explain.

May Journal Suggestions

- May is Revise Your Work Schedule Month. Describe your plans to work smarter, not harder, at your schoolwork.

- Older Americans Month is celebrated in May. What is the most important thing an older person has taught you? Explain how it has benefited you.

- May is National High Blood Pressure Education Month. What causes your blood pressure to rise? Why?

- May is Better Hearing and Speech Month. Describe in detail three things you are most likely to "tune out" and not hear.

- Jockey Diane Crump became the first woman to ride in the Kentucky Derby in May of 1970. What "first" would you like to become noted for and why?

- May 3 is International Tuba Day. Do you think all kids should be required to take music lessons? Justify your reasons.

- Horace Mann, who became the "Father of the Public School System," was born on May 4, 1796. Explain how you would change your school if you could.

- People are encouraged to collect and send picture postcards during National Postcard Week, held the first full week in May. Describe the location in your town that would make the best picture-postcard photograph.

- National Teacher Appreciation Week is observed annually the first full week in May. Describe an ideal teacher. Do you think you have those qualities? Do you think teachers should be replaced by computers or TVs? Explain your answer.

- May 8 is No Socks Day. What other stuff would you like to omit, skip, or ignore for a day?

- Mother's Day is celebrated on the second Sunday in May. Think of a famous mom you would like to adopt for a week. Describe how you would spend your time together.

- Gabriel Fahrenheit, the inventor of the mercury thermometer, was born on May 14, 1686. Are you usually a cool cucumber or a hothead? Explain.

- On May 16, 1868, the impeachment of President Andrew Johnson failed by one vote. What would you say to a person who told you he has never voted in a presidential election and never will?

- May 16 is Biographers Day. Whose biography would you most like to write? Why?

June Journal Suggestions

- June marks the beginning of summer vacation for kids in many parts of the country. What do you plan to do on the first day of your vacation? Why?

- June is often thought of as the month for weddings. What do you think is the ideal age for getting married? Why?

- When Michael Kearney was only ten years old, he graduated in from the University of South Alabama. What would be the advantages and disadvantages of graduating from college at such a young age?

Gee, it's my graduation, and I can't see anything!

- National Fragrance Week is celebrated the first full week in June. If you were blindfolded, what smells would let you know that you were at home and not someplace else?

- Charles Richard Drew—born on June 3, 1904—set up the world's first blood bank at the American Red Cross. If you had a seriously ill friend in the hospital who needed a blood transfusion, what would you say to him?

- On June 6, 1933, the first drive-in movie theater opened in Camden, New Jersey. If you could change two things about movies today, what would you change? Why?

- June 6—the birthdate of the American patriot Nathan Hale—marks the beginning of National Patriots Month. Explain what you think a patriot is. Are you a patriot? Why or why not?

I only regret that I have but one life to lose for my country... Oh yeah, and I regret not turning in those library books, too.

- Two well-known cartoon characters were "born" in June—Donald Duck on the 9th and Garfield on the 19th. What kind of cartoon character do you think will be invented next? Explain.

- When George Bush (who was born on June 12, 1924) was president, his pet dog Millie lived in the White House with him and his family. Other presidents have had a turkey and a garter snake as pets! If you could choose a pet for the current president, what would you choose, and why?

SLURRRRP!!!

- June 14 is Flag Day. If you had to design your own personal flag, what symbols would it include? Why?

- Father's Day is celebrated the third Sunday in June. If you could give tips to all the dads in the world on how to get along better with their kids, what would you tell them?

- Helen Keller's birth anniversary is June 27. She once said, "Science may have found a cure for most evils; but it has found no remedy for the worst of them all—the apathy of human beings." Look up *apathy* in a dictionary. Tell why you agree or disagree with Ms. Keller.

- The school year is drawing to an end. As you reflect on it, what was the highest point of your year? Explain.

- Summer vacation often means it's time for family reunions. What's the funniest thing that's ever happened when your family has gotten together for a special occasion?

July Journal Suggestions

- July is National Hot Dog Month. Describe a time when you acted like a real "hot dog."

- Anti-Boredom Month is observed in July. What are your best suggestions for fighting boredom?

- The first zoo in the United States opened in Philadelphia on July 1, 1874. How do you feel about zoos keeping wild animals on exhibit?

- July 1 is the anniversary of the Battle Of Gettysburg, which was fought in 1863. How would life in the United States be different if the South had won the Civil War?

- On July 2, exactly 1/2 of the year will have passed. Which of your New Year's resolutions have you kept? What goals do you plan to work on for the rest of the year?

- Music For Life Week is observed the first full week of July. Name your favorite type of music. How does this music make your life better?

- The first Black American Supreme Court justice, Thurgood Marshall, was born on July 2, 1908. What unusual problems might a person who was *first* to accomplish something face? What personal attributes do you think would help that person deal with these problems?

- On July 2, 1964, President Lyndon B. Johnson signed the Voting Rights Act of 1964. Why do you think so few people exercise their right to vote? How can we change that?

- The first full week in July is Be Nice To New Jersey Week—sponsored to recognize the positive aspects of this state. What good things about your state would you like to share with others in the United States?

- The first U.S. bank opened in New York City on July 3, 1819. Do you consider yourself a saver or a spender? Explain.

- Compliment-Your-Mirror Day is celebrated on July 3. What are the best features of the face that smiles at you in the mirror each morning?

- Esther Pauline Friedman—better known as the advice columnist Ann Landers—was born on July 4, 1918. Whom do you know that could most benefit from her advice right now? Explain.

- Talk show host Geraldo Rivera celebrates his birthday on July 4. What qualities do you think a good talk show host must have?

- Babe Ruth was honored with a commemorative postage stamp on July 6, 1983. What will you have accomplished when a commemorative stamp is issued in *your* honor?

Patterns

Use the journal cover art with the ideas on pages 49–50 and 51–52.

Note To The Teacher: Duplicate this page on white construction paper for each student. Instruct students to cut their copies in half on the dividing line. Have students decorate their August covers; then have each child staple several sheets of lined paper (cut to size) behind his cover. Save the September covers to use for September journals.

Use the journal cover art with the ideas on pages 53–54 and 55–56.

Note To The Teacher: Duplicate this page on white construction paper for each student. Instruct students to cut their copies in half on the dividing line. Have students decorate their October covers; then have each child staple several sheets of lined paper (cut to size) behind his cover. Save the November covers to use for November journals.

Use the journal cover art with the ideas on pages 57–58 and 59–60.

Note To The Teacher: Duplicate this page on white construction paper for each student. Instruct students to cut their copies in half on the dividing line. Have students decorate their December covers; then have each child staple several sheets of lined paper (cut to size) behind his cover. Save the January covers to use for January journals.

Use the journal cover art with the ideas on pages 61–62 and 63–64.

Note To The Teacher: Duplicate this page on white construction paper for each student. Instruct students to cut their copies in half on the dividing line. Have students decorate their February covers; then have each child staple several sheets of lined paper (cut to size) behind his cover. Save the March covers to use for March journals.

Use the journal cover art with the ideas on pages 65–66 and 67–68.

Note To The Teacher: Duplicate this page on white construction paper for each student. Instruct students to cut their copies in half on the dividing line. Have students decorate their April covers; then have each child staple several sheets of lined paper (cut to size) behind his cover. Save the May covers to use for May journals.

Use the journal cover art with the ideas on pages 69 and 70.

Note To The Teacher: Duplicate this page on white construction paper for each student. Instruct students to cut their copies in half on the dividing line. Have students decorate their June covers; then have each child staple several sheets of lined paper cut to size behind his cover. Save the July covers to use for July journals.

Write On!

Ideas And Tips For Teaching Students To Write!

Five Dollars For Your Thoughts

At the beginning of each year, I have students complete a short written assignment that begins with this starter: "If I had five dollars, I would buy…." This activity gives me a quick overview of student writing skills, as well as a list of things that I might use as motivators and rewards throughout the upcoming year.

Summer Tucker—Special Education, Special Learning Center, Knoxville, TN

"In-spidered" Writing

"In-spider" your students to write this fall with the help of some eight-legged friends! Duplicate a spider pattern on black construction paper for each student. Give each student a spider and a piece of white chalk, directing him to write one writing topic on each leg of his spider. Next have each student cut out his spider and add wiggle or cut-out eyes to it. Draw a web outline on a covered bulletin board and post the spiders on it. Use an inexpensive, cotton spiderweb for a more authentic look. Encourage students to refer to the spiders for future writing inspiration.

Julie Eick Granchelli—Gr. 4, Towne Elementary, Medina, NY

It's All In The Details

Here's another idea to improve descriptive writing skills. As a homework assignment, instruct each student to write a description of his bed. Collect all writings the next day. Then randomly distribute each description to a student other than its author. Each student reads the description that he receives and illustrates the bed, based on the details. The bed owner's name is also written on the back of the illustration. When everyone is finished, display all the illustrations on a bulletin board. Then ask volunteers, one at a time, to try and identify their beds from the illustrations. Students quickly realize not only the need for specific details and color in their writing, but also the importance of putting details in order. This activity can be done using coats, backpacks, T-shirts, athletic shoes, or any items common to all students.

Diane Rhodes, Dudley Gifted and Talented Magnet School, Victoria, TX

Big Books For Little Ones

Want a project that will get your students into writing? I had my reading class work in cooperative groups to produce giant books for kindergartners. We used extra-large paper for the pages and sentence strips for the text. The students brainstormed topic ideas in their groups. A text was written by each group, then approved by me. The groups decided how illustrations would be completed and what media to use. Some children made pop-out pictures; others used chalk or paint. The pages were hole-punched and bound with yarn. The production of the books was a wonderful experience. The younger children were delighted, and the giant books were a nice contribution to the kindergarten library!

Sr. Ann Claire Rhoads, St. Pius X Catholic School, Greensboro, NC

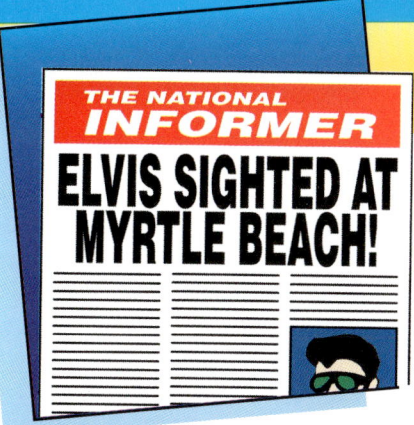

Terrific Tabloids

Inspire creative writing with an unlikely resource: supermarket tabloids! Purchase a few scandal sheets that have interesting stories. Clip appropriate headlines and distribute them to your students. They'll have a great time writing and illustrating stories with such titles as "I Was Bigfoot's Baby" and "Aliens Think Earth Is A Bad Neighborhood"! Display students' compositions and drawings on a bulletin board backed with newspapers.

Jennifer Suhling—Gr. 4, Reeces Creek Elementary, Killeen, TX

A Pet Book

A pet in the classroom is a real hit for starting out a new year. My fourth graders invite a first-grade class to join us in a learning project on our pet. After students read and discuss both fiction and nonfiction books about the animal, we brainstorm everything that we learned about it. We use other media, such as slides and tapes, to gain even more information. Students then create a big book about the animal. A first grader and a fourth grader work as partners to create each page. Together they decide what they want to include on their page; then the fourth grader writes the words, while both students work together on the illustrations. Completed pages are laminated and bound into a big book that is displayed in the media center and shared with the whole school. This project is a wonderful one with which to begin the year. It motivates students in both grades and promotes a spirit of friendship that we build on throughout the year.

Carmelle L. Lamothe—Gr. 4, Jewett Street Elementary, Manchester, NH

Pint-Size Adventures

Inspired by *The Borrowers* by Mary Norton, I asked my students to "borrow" small items from their homes—items that they might consider useless. In small groups, students brainstormed the various ways in which little people, such as the Borrowers, might put these items to good use. Each student then wrote an adventure story to share with the class.

Pamela Mckedy—Resource, Highland Falls Middle School, Highland Falls, NY

Principal For A Day

My school holds a Principal For A Day contest. To be eligible, every student in grades three through six writes about what it would be like to be the principal. Each homeroom teacher chooses five top essays, from which the students select a class winner. Grade-level winners are chosen by a panel of teachers. Each winner takes a turn being principal for a day. Some of the principal's duties include sorting and distributing the mail, running errands, supervising the cafeteria, and writing letters for the secretary to type. Everyone loves having the chance to be principal for a day. This idea can easily be adapted to a Teacher For A Day contest.

Linda Warner, Bath Elementary, Akron, OH

Synonym Trees

A pair of synonym trees are just the thing for students whose writing is growing short on word variety! Cut two large tree trunks—each with six large branches—from brown bulletin-board paper. Attach the trees to a classroom wall; then cut a generous supply of leaves from fall-colored construction paper. Next have your students brainstorm a list of words they feel are overused in their writing, such as *big, said,* and *good.* Instruct students to select the 12 most overused words from the list. Record each of the selected words on a tree branch; then direct students to use a thesaurus to find and share aloud synonyms for each overused word. Record each synonym on a cut-out leaf and attach it to the branch of the word it can replace. Remind each student to refer to the trees for a synonym whenever he finds himself stumped!

Nancy Oglevie Jaeger—Gr. 5, Sangre Ridge Elementary, Stillwater, OK

Paper-Bag Busts

Motivating even your most reluctant writers is in the bag with this creative-writing activity! Instruct each student to research a famous person or character. Then have him construct a bust of that person using a small paper lunch bag and various art materials. After completing his bag bust, have each student write a poem, paragraph, or rhyming riddle about his character's identity. Finally allow each student to share his bag and writing with the class.

Donna Brasher—Gr. 4
Cherokee Elementary
Guntersville, AL

Rough Drafts On Yellow

Eliminate confusion between works in progress and final copies with the following idea. At the beginning of the school year, ask each student to contribute a yellow legal pad to the classroom. Have students use the yellow paper for writing rough drafts and editing. The extra length of these pads provides more space for making changes. After all editing and revisions are complete, have students write their final copies on white composition paper.

Nancy Curl—Gr. 6
Olson Middle School
Tabernacle, NJ

Monthly Management

Looking for an easy way to manage your writing program? Tired of endless student drafts and revisions with no perfected final product? Then try this management strategy! Begin by choosing eight writing themes, one for each month of the school year. Next choose two skills and one part of speech to emphasize throughout each monthly theme. Create a chart as shown and provide each student with a copy. Direct each student to take her monthly writing piece through all stages of the writing process. At the end of the year, each child will have at least eight written masterpieces in her portfolio!

	September	October	November
Monthly Theme	Letters	Autobiographies	Interviewing
Skill 1	parts of a letter	sequencing	questioning
Skill 2	paragraphs	expressing thoughts, feelings	researching
Part Of Speech	nouns	verbs	adjectives
Perfected Product	letter	autobiography	family history album

Ben Fromuth—Gr. 4, Penrose Elementary, Colorado Springs, CO

Shoebox Stories

To generate ideas for cooperative writing, fill shoeboxes with trinkets, gadgets, small toys, and other intriguing items. Give a box to each group. Have each group member examine the box's contents and then write a story, paragraph, or poem about the objects. After groups have used each box once, empty the boxes and mix the items for another round of super student stories.

Deedra Bignar—Gr. 6, Nebo Elementary, Jena, LA

Work Under Construction

Frustrated with the way your writers lose their work? As writing workshop ends each day, have students tack their unfinished projects on a board titled "Work Under Construction." Allow students to survey their classmates' work during breaks and attach positive comments written on Post-It® Brand notes to them. Students love reading their peers' comments, and I love knowing where their papers really are!

Christine Smyth—Gr. 5, Hanson Elementary, Buxton, ME

Pumpkin Pals

My students enjoyed the following autumn writing/art activity. First the students created giant pumpkin heads from recycled, brown-paper grocery bags. Each student painted her bag orange. The bag was then stuffed with newspaper, gathered at the top, and tied to create a "stem." Students used construction paper to add distinctive facial features, turning their pumpkin heads into unique characters. Finally each student wrote a story about how her pumpkin pal came to be in school. The published stories and attractive pumpkins made a humorous harvest display.

Ana Byrd—K–5 Gifted, Miami Shores Elementary, Miami Shores, FL

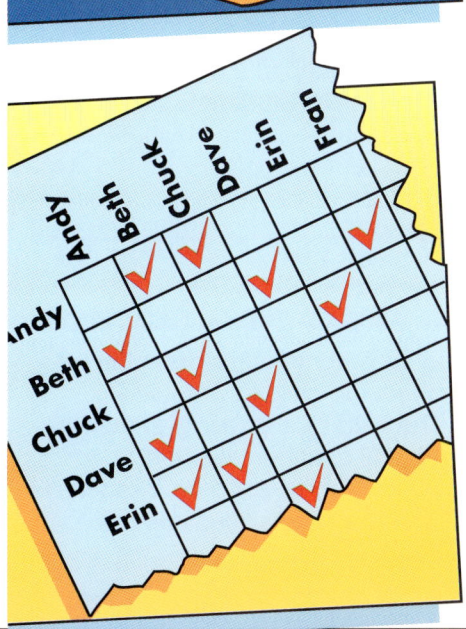

November Letter Writing

Begin each November morning with a letter-writing activity that's sure to enhance the meaning of Thanksgiving. Have each student decorate a paper lunch bag with a fall or Thanksgiving scene. Write each student's name on the front of her bag. Then tape the bags in alphabetical order on a wall.

Next review the parts of a friendly letter with students. Ask each student to write a letter to another student expressing why she is thankful for him/her. Then have the student "mail" the letter by slipping it into that person's mailbox (decorated bag). Explain that students will repeat this activity every day for several weeks, writing to a different classmate each morning. Display an incentive chart as shown. Demonstrate how the chart will help students keep track of the letters they write so they won't send two letters to the same person. Allow time each Friday for reading the mail.

Melissa M. Jones—Gr. 4, Waynesville Elementary, Waynesville, OH

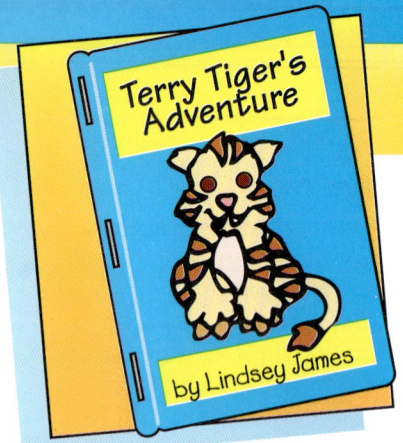

Stuffed Animal Books

After reading *The Velveteen Rabbit,* I was inspired with this writing activity. I asked each child to bring an old stuffed animal that he would be willing to give to the library. Each child then wrote a story about his animal. The stories were edited and published as individual books. We then used Velcro to attach each student's animal to the front cover of his book. Each child made an author, title, and subject card to be placed in the card catalog in the library. Students read their books to kindergarten, first-, and second-grade classes. We then placed each book and animal in the library for general checkout. My students felt quite proud to have created such popular library books.

Florence Melda—Gr. 4, Jasper Elementary, Jasper, GA

Students' Published Stories Rack

Realizing that my students weren't getting the opportunity to share their finished stories with each other, I created a "magazine rack" for displaying their published work. To make the rack, I used a sheet of large poster board colored on both sides, clear packaging tape, and thin ribbon cut two inches longer than the length of the poster board. I folded the poster board lengthwise about two-thirds of the way up to create a giant pocket. Then I taped the ends securely. I stretched the ribbon lengthwise across the upper part of the poster and secured the ribbon to the back with tape. Papers fit neatly into the folded portion of the rack and were held upright by the ribbon. I added signs that read "Hot Off The Press," "From Miss Halleran's Publishing Company," and "Please Read!"; then I hung the display on my classroom door. Now students from all over the school enjoy stopping by my classroom to read the stories displayed in the rack.

Robin Halleran—Gr. 5, Livingston Elementary, Covington, GA

Student Editors

Help students identify their peer editors during writing workshop in a jiffy. Have each editor wear a colorful and inexpensive plastic visor labeled "Student Editor." Students will no longer have to keep up with who the editors are—it'll be obvious!

Debbie Patrick—Gr. 5, Park Forest Elementary, State College, PA

Alphabet Sentences

Encourage elaboration with wishful thinking! First have each student brainstorm a list of objects that he would like to have. After selecting his favorite object from the list, have the student draw a picture of his object. Then instruct the child to write sentences describing what he would do with that object. The catch is that every sentence must begin with a new letter of the alphabet. For example, if a student wanted a horse, he might write, "If I had a horse, I would…**A**lways be happy, **B**uy him a saddle, **C**atch him and ride him, etc." As a final product, publish the students' ideas as alphabet books.

Sandy Hawkins, Richmond Elementary, Fleetwood, PA

Halloween With A Twist

Challenge students to expand their word power with this Halloween writing twist. First have students brainstorm a list of "scary" words, as you list them on the chalkboard. Instruct them to think about the words that they encounter in spooky stories or ones that they often hear when watching scary movies. After you've listed about 15 of the words most often mentioned, instruct each student to write a Halloween story—without using any of the words listed on the board. Challenge students to use dictionaries or thesauruses to discover new and different synonyms for the words they want to use. Be sure to provide a sharing time for students to read their compositions.

Serving Up Some Thanks

Serve up a creative writing challenge with this colorful turkey. To make, staple together two sturdy paper plates. Write the letters of the alphabet on colorful paper feathers and insert them into the stapled plates. Add a head, legs, feet, and any other desired details to complete the turkey. Have each student "pluck a feather" from the turkey. The student lists as many items that she is thankful for as possible, all beginning with the letter on the feather.

Beth Besley, Nashua, NH

"Classy" Mail

A classroom Mail Center provides plenty of creative writing opportunities for my students. To make the center, cut the ends from the shoeboxes (one per student) and stack them to create a mailbox for each child. Label each box with a student's name. At a nearby center, place paper scraps, typing paper, rubber ink stamps, colorful inkpads, stickers, and other writing materials. When students have free time, they can create stationery, bookmarks, greeting cards, postcards, and letters to mail to their classmates. You'll be pleasantly surprised as students write, write, and write! I also use the Mail Center to send notes to students. I try to make sure that each child receives a special note from me at least once a week.

Debbie Moreno—Gr. 5, Santa Fe Intermediate School, League City, TX

Newsworthy Descriptions

Enhance descriptive writing skills with this simple activity. From a newspaper, cut a picture of an everyday object or figure, such as a golfer, jogger, auto, food, or soft drink. Have a student study the picture and then give an oral description to the rest of the class. Encourage the student to describe the object well enough for his classmates to guess its identity.

As a cooperative activity, have groups of students work together to write descriptions of pictures. Then have the groups try to identify each other's objects or figures from the written descriptions.

Diana Curtis, Albuquerque, NM

Pass It To Parents

All it takes is one minute a week for me to involve parents in my writing program. I divide my students into groups of five. On Monday one student from each group writes the beginning of a story. At the end of the day, he takes the story starter home in a decorated folder; then he has a parent (or grandparent) add to the story, writing for only one minute. The student returns the story to school the next day and passes it to the second child in his group. That student adds to the tale and takes it home for his family's addition. By the end of the week, each student and his family have helped to write a terrific story. We type the finished stories into our computer and make copies to send home. Parents and kids alike love the results of this fun project.

Linda Sherbinsky, Chesapeake, VA

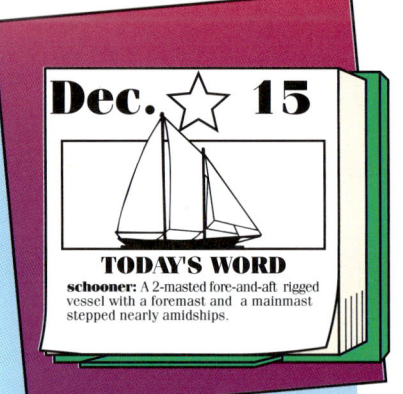

Word-A-Day Calendars

Early in the New Year when prices are reduced, I buy an inexpensive word-a-day calendar. Ignoring the dates, my students study two or three new words each week. (At this rate, one calendar lasts several years!) We discuss the definition of each word, and students share sentences in which they use it. Then each student writes a definition of the word and a sample sentence in his journal. (I often write an introductory phrase for students who have difficulty composing sentences.) To help students remember these calendar words, I display a running list (computer generated) in the classroom.

Denise Amos—Gr. 4, Crestwood Elementary, Crestwood, KY

Look Who's Writing To Santa!

Social studies, research, and letter writing—your students can hit on all three with this fun activity! Have each student choose a historical figure from your social studies units. Pretending to be that person, the student writes a letter to Santa Claus, asking for things that the person might actually have wanted and needed. Students then add illustrations to their letters. A great project to wrap up a literature unit on biographies too!

Julie Alarie—Gr. 6, Essex Middle School, Essex, VT

A Time Of Sharing

As the holidays approach, try this cooperative writing/art project. Divide students into groups of four. Provide each student with a sheet of drawing paper and instruct her to draw a holiday picture. After five minutes—without warning—have each student pass her drawing to the group member on her right. Continue until each child in the group has contributed to all four pictures. Collect the drawings; then return them the next day, instructing each student to write a story about her picture. After five minutes—without warning—stop the students and instruct them to pass their stories to the right. Again each group member contributes to each story. When each story returns to its owner, she finishes it and makes any corrections. I display all of these stories and illustrations on a bulletin board titled "A Time Of Sharing."

Ann Redmond—Gr. 4, Lower Salford Elementary, Harleysville, PA

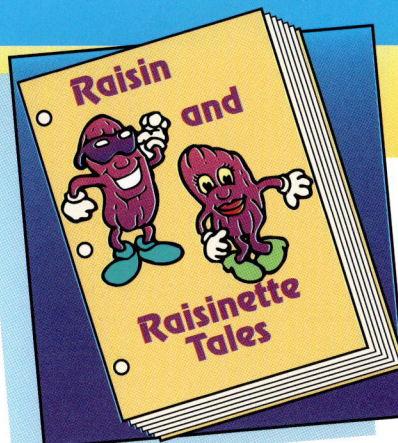

Class Publishing

One year I welcomed whole language into my room with a class publishing venture. My students first agreed on a topic on which everyone would write a story. Since they were so popular at the time, students enthusiastically elected to write stories about the California Raisins. Each child used the computer to compose his story; then the story was edited by a classmate. After being printed, the story was edited again by me and another classmate. Some students drew pictures to illustrate their stories. Completed pages were numbered, laminated, and bound together in a class book. It was a project that taught a multitude of skills and raised my students' self-esteem.

Dr. Rebecca Webster Graves—Academically Gifted, Burlington City Schools, Burlington, NC

Seasonal Story Starters

'Tis the season for some holiday writing fun! Write each of the following ideas on a large, construction paper ornament; then staple it on a bulletin board Christmas tree.
- Invent a new way for Santa to travel on Christmas Eve.
- Make a list of items which can fit inside an average-sized stocking.
- List the advantages and disadvantages of live and artificial Christmas trees.
- Write a story that explains why candy canes have stripes.
- Mrs. Claus never gets credit for her hard work! Write a speech honoring Mrs. Claus and the jobs she does for her husband.
- Write a news story describing a "Santa Sighting" by a pilot who was flying on Christmas Eve.
- Santa got stuck in your chimney. How would you help him get out without injury?

Chris Christensen—Gr. 4, Doris Hancock Elementary School, Las Vegas, NV

Out-Of-Work Elves

My students will never forget an unusual writing assignment we did at Christmas last year. I had students pretend that they were out-of-work elves applying for jobs at Santa's workshop. Each student listed his previous work experience, his strengths and weaknesses, and a list of references. To practice letter-writing, I had the student write a letter from each of his references to send along with his application. I even had a parent volunteer come to school dressed as Santa to interview the most promising applicants!

Lisa Stone—Gr. 5, Reno, NV

Famous Resolutions

Ring in the new year with a fun creative-writing assignment! Have each student label a slip of paper with the name of a well-known person or book character. Put the slips in a box. Have each child draw a name; then have him write a list of new year's resolutions he thinks the person he drew would make. What fun!

Chris Christensen—Gr. 4

Pen Pal Pair Up

Writing to pen pals is a fun way to practice letter-writing skills and develop new friendships. Corresponding with pen pals can be even easier when you pair up with a teacher in your own school system. You'll save money and time, since the letters can be delivered by the system's courier service. As an added bonus, plan a field trip to visit your pen pals at their school, or invite them to yours. It's a great end-of-the-year trip!

Julie B. Ferrara, N. B. Cook School, Pensacola, FL

Punny Valentines

For a creative holiday writing project, have your students try a little "Valentine Pun Fun." Display some valentines for students to read, noting how puns are frequently used in their messages. Then provide art paper for your students to create their own valentines, incorporating puns somewhere in them. You'll be surprised at the clever messages that kids will come up with—no "lion"!

Sr. Ann Claire Rhodes, St. Pius X School, Greensboro, NC

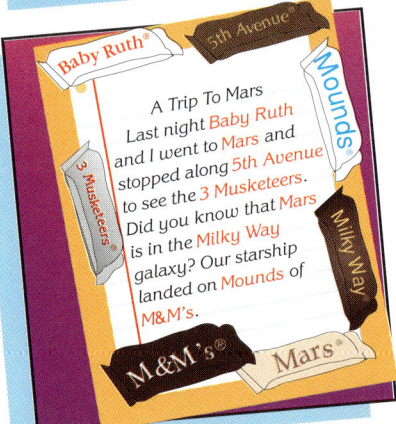

Candy Wrapper Writings

My classroom was all smiles over a creative writing activity that I call "Bar Mania." My sixth graders were asked to sign up for their favorite candy bars. On a set day, everyone was instructed to bring his chosen candy bar to class, and we all enjoyed a delicious snack! (It's a good idea to let parents know that the candy is part of a writing assignment!) After the candies were eaten, I pinned all the wrappers to the bulletin board. Each student was then instructed to write a story incorporating all of the candy names. For example, one story included this sentence: "Last night, *Baby Ruth* and I went to *Mars* and stopped along *5th Avenue* to see the *3 Musketeers*." For emphasis, the candy names were written in large print or in color. Then the students paired up to proofread each other's stories. After rewriting, final copies were displayed on a bulletin board entitled "Bar Mania." Candy wrappers were attached between the stories and around the border. These stories turned out to be the most creative my students have ever written. Even my reluctant readers eagerly awaited the due date!

Tammie Kay McClure—Gr. 6, Tryon Elementary, Gastonia, NC

Cartoon Creations

Intermediate kids love comic strips! For a writing activity, I glue comic strips and cartoons to construction paper, adding creative and critical thinking questions for the readers to answer. This idea works very well with my reluctant readers and writers, and can be adapted for any grade level.

Anne Runyon—Gr. 5, Littleton, CO

Terrific Teacher Journal

I've learned that while it's important for a teacher to read when children are reading, it's equally important to write when they're writing. So the latest addition to my bookshelf is a writing journal. Whenever my students write, so do I! I jot down ideas to share with colleagues, funny sayings, and classroom happenings. During this time I also revise, edit, and prepare my rough copy. I even share some of my writing with my students, who love to hear about themselves. In the summer, I type final copies of my ideas and send them to *The Mailbox®!*

Ann Redmond—Gr. 4, Lower Salford Elementary School, Harleysville, PA

Cooperative Paragraphs

Cooperative paragraphs are a great way to encourage thinking and strengthen writing skills. Instruct each student to write a topic sentence. The sentence should express the main idea of a paragraph on any familiar topic, such as a TV show, teacher, sport, movie, musician, or food. All papers are then passed to the right, front, back, or left, so that each student receives a classmate's topic sentence. Each receiver reads the sentence and adds a detail sentence to support it. Papers are then passed in the same direction three more times, with students adding supporting details to each paragraph they receive. After the fourth exchange, the paragraphs are read aloud. This activity is perfect for any content area review. For example, assign "The American Revolution had many heroes" or "The wheel and axle have many uses" as a topic sentence.

Jan Shaffer—Gr. 5, Brentwood School, Plainfield, IN

Noteworthy Address

Keep a file of important and often-used addresses in your writing center. Include addresses of the president and other government officials, your principal, area businesses, zoos, authors, and students. You can even add your own. Students will love going to the file and choosing addresses of people or organizations to write to. It's a great way to encourage letter-writing skills!

Kay W. Bindrim—Gr. 6–7 Chapter I, Parker Middle School, Rocky Mount, NC

Sticky Stories

Everyone in class earns a sticker with this creative writing activity! Give each child a sticker which has a character on it. The student attaches the sticker to his paper and writes a narrative story about the character. Each story must have a setting and plot that are related to the sticker. The child can include other characters in the story as well. This is a great opportunity to reinforce the concepts of plot, setting, and character. It also gives students a chance to sharpen creative writing skills.

Sue Lynch—Gr. 4, Morgan Woods Elementary School, Tampa, FL

Editing Made Easy

To keep track of where each of my students is in the writing process, I developed a simple tracking system using the chalkboard, an animal-shaped notepad, and some magnetic tape. I wrote each child's name on a note, laminated it, and attached a piece of magnetic tape to the back. I then divided my chalkboard into four columns—first draft, edit, final draft, and completed work. Each student begins a writing assignment with his name under the first draft column and moves his marker as he progresses through the writing process. When the student reaches the editing phase, I call him up to conference individually. Now I no longer have a line of students at my desk waiting for help.

Jan Dempsey, Jefferson Elementary, West Allis, WI

Kiss And Tell

A bag of Hershey's Kisses® is all you need for this fun and tasty writing activity. Give each student a piece of candy and have her record the following information in a descriptive paragraph:
- how the kiss looks
- how to unwrap the candy
- how the candy feels on her tongue
- the taste as she eats the candy

After students have finished their writing, have volunteers share their work. For variety, try another type of candy or even a dill pickle slice if you really want to grab their attention!

Lelia Van Meter—Gr. 5, Sabine Elementary, Gladewater, TX

Leap Into Leprechaun Writing

Liven up your St. Patrick's Day celebration with the following writing activity. Write the boldfaced information from the following list on the chalkboard without telling students what they will be writing about:

1. **an animal** — *leprechaun's pet*
2. **a color** — *color he wears*
3. **a kind of transportation** — *his transportation*
4. **a place** — *setting of story*
5. **a food** — *his favorite food*
6. **a name** — *leprechaun's name*

Ask your students to number a piece of paper from one to six and record a response for each item. After your students have written their responses, post the italicized information on the board. Inform your students that they will use their recorded responses and the new information to write a story about a leprechaun. Bind the finished stories into a class book.

Candy Whelan, Garlough Elementary, West St. Paul, MN

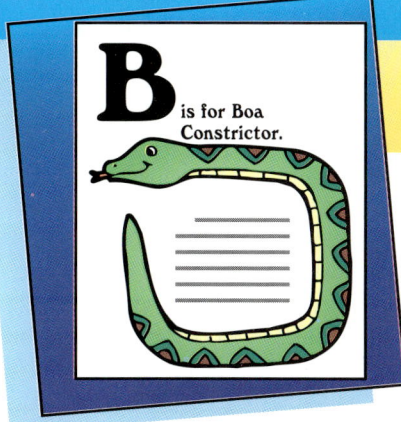

A Year Of Writing From A To Z

Try this terrific, year-end writing activity with your intermediate students. Have each student prepare a booklet of poetry and prose writings, one for each letter of the alphabet. For example: a poem that uses alliteration for the letter *A*, an expository paragraph on boa constrictors for the letter *B*, and a cinquain on the *C* page. *A* to *Z* booklets provide an excellent review of writing skills learned during the year and stimulate students' creative thinking. They're also priceless treasures for both students and their parents.

Angela Guthrie—Gr. 5, Bluff Park Elementary, Birmingham, AL

"Lewie's Great Escape"

My students love to write stories about Lewie, our class's pet rabbit. To get students started, I take pictures of Lewie in such places as a teacher's mailbox, the gym, a bathroom sink, and on the principal's desk; then I post the photos in the classroom. Students use the photos as springboards for their stories, which they title "Lewie's Great Escape." I display the completed stories and the photos in a hallway for the enjoyment of the entire school. Adapt this fun writing activity for any classroom pet or even a stuffed animal.

Kathy Galford—Gr. 5, Greenbrier Intermediate School, Chesapeake, VA

Just Look At Us!

After reading numerous biographies and autobiographies of famous Americans, my students can't wait to publish their own life stories. Using computer software, I produce an "All About Me" page with spaces for autobiographical information, such as personal description, family, embarrassing moments, interests, influential people, and lifetime goals. Students fill out these pages with family photos, anecdotes, and quotes. The sketches are shared orally and then mounted on paper and bound in a binder bearing the title "Just Look At Us!"

Geralyn P. Smitherman—Gr. 4, Youens Elementary, Houston, TX

Character Riddle Book

As a year-end project, my students publish a class book that focuses on memorable book characters. We first brainstorm and list favorite characters from books read during the year. I post this list throughout the project. The entire class then collaboratively creates several riddles about the characters, which I write on a transparency. I demonstrate how adjectives and verbs make the riddles more interesting. Students then write their own riddles and discuss them with each other. After revisions and editing, I type the students' riddles and an answer key. Copies are made and compiled into class books, one for each child. This is a fun, creative way to guide students through the writing process.

Mary Ly Lowen, Lipstreu Elementary, Springtown, TX

Bottled Messages

Allow a sense of adventure, mystery, and intrigue to invade your next writing lesson. Pen a brief message on a white piece of paper, roll it up, and place it inside a clear, plastic bottle. Inform the class that you found the bottle over the weekend at the seashore (or on the bank of a nearby lake) but have not yet examined its contents. Lead the class in a discussion about the bottle's contents. Explore ideas about where the bottle was found and how it got there. Predict what the note inside might say, and who might have written it and why. Could it be a pirate's treasure map? Or a note from someone who is in trouble? Encourage the students to let their imaginations run wild as they complete this creative-writing assignment, but don't forget to finally reveal the mysterious message inside!

LaDawn Rhodes—Gr. 4, Shelton Park Elementary, Virginia Beach, VA

Life Without Me

Need a pick-me-up kind of creative-writing idea? Fill a brown grocery bag with items picked up from around your classroom. (Suggested items: pen, ruler, book, eraser, glue bottle, paper clip, notebook paper, roll of tape, stapler, chalk, etc.) Allow each student to reach inside the sack and pull out one item. Then challenge him to write about his life without this item and tell whether he would be able to cope. Also challenge him to elaborate on whether the item could be replaced with something else. Have each student draw a larger-than-life outline of his item on which to copy his story; then post the cutouts for an instant bulletin board!

Doreen Placko, Antioch School System, Antioch, IL

Writing Is My Bag!

Post this quick-and-easy, anytime bulletin board to motivate writing! Collect a variety of colorful bags from different businesses and restaurants in your area. Staple the bags to a bulletin board so that they hang open. Have students write about their personal experiences when visiting these places. Or instruct them to include information about these places when writing original stories. Have each student roll up his completed story and place it in a bag. Students can then pull out and read each other's stories.

Nancy Rafay, Bartlett, TX

Recognizing Bias

Do your students recognize biased writing? Can they differentiate fact from opinion? Cut out about 30 magazine pictures of people (avoiding any famous personalities). Have each student choose a picture and follow these steps:

1. Imagine that the individual pictured is someone to be admired.
   Write a brief paragraph biased in favor of that person.
2. Pretend that the person pictured is someone not to be admired.
   Write a short paragraph biased against the person in the picture.
3. Study your picture and write a factual paragraph about the person.

Afterwards, ask volunteers to share their pictures with the class and read aloud one of his paragraphs; then have their classmates determine if the paragraph is factual, biased for the person, or biased against the person. This is a wonderful way to help students evaluate bias in each other's writing.

Elsie B. McGill—Grs. 6–8, College Park Middle School, Hickory, NC

Book Of Memories

Make the end of the year extra special by reflecting on what made the entire year extra special! I instruct my class to write about the activities of the past year that were the most fun. Students prewrite, edit, and rewrite, following the usual writing process. Each student is then given a duplicating master on which he writes and illustrates his final copy. All of the masters are duplicated; then copies are distributed to every member of the class. Each student makes covers and assembles his pages into a booklet. A time is provided for students to sign each other's booklets. Everyone, including my assistant and me, then has a special *Book Of Memories*. I'll treasure mine forever!

Barbara Mueller—Gr. 3 & 4 Special Education, West Buncombe Elementary School, Asheville, NC

End-Of-Year Storytelling

Students in our school save all of their writings throughout the year. Near the end of the year, every student in the fourth grade chooses a favorite story from his collection to share. The entire grade level is then regrouped so that new audiences get to listen to the stories. Afterwards we celebrate with a treat of punch and cookies. This grade-level activity works especially well during the last week of school. It provides a different, fun activity for everyone. Plus it's an exciting way to celebrate a year's growth as authors.

Debbie Easterday—Gr. 4, Skyview Elementary, Thornton, CO

Amiable Autographs

Children can easily get into a habit of using put-downs with each other. Year-end autograph booklets provide them with an opportunity to write kind and complimentary comments about their classmates. I provide each student with enough lined pages to create a page per classmate. When they are completed, the pages are distributed to the students. I provide time for assembling the pages into booklets and designing covers. These autograph booklets are a terrific way to get children to validate one another and, at the same time, to provide valuable writing experiences.

Alice N. Rice, Scottsdale, AZ

An Audience With Authors

My young authors are always proud of their original poems and stories. Their writings are beautifully illustrated and usually take a great deal of time. To show appreciation for the students' efforts, I invite parents into our classroom on the last day of school for a Writing Celebration. All of the children's writings that I saved during the year are displayed in the classroom for parents' viewing and reading pleasure. Each child also chooses her favorite piece to read to the audience. Refreshments are served, and both students and their families are thrilled by a very special celebration.

Patricia Shulman—Gr. 5, Hillside School, Needham, MA

Group Puppet Plays

Take it from Punch and Judy—puppet shows are always a hit, even with intermediate kids! For a fun group writing activity, I give each student a small paper sack and instructions to create a unique puppet character. After the puppets are finished, I divide the class into groups of three or four; then I direct each group to write a play that incorporates the puppets of its members. The combinations of characters—animals, community helpers, and even superheroes—always generate lots of laughs! After the students write their group plays, they perform them for one another. Writing, art, cooperation, and presentation skills are all wrapped up in one fun lesson!

Cathy Wallace—Gr. 4, Glendale, AZ

Lost At Sea!

Whether you're studying the ocean or just looking for a unique writing activity, take a tip from Gilligan and head out to sea! For each student, use masking tape to make a large rectangle (big enough to sit in) on your classroom floor. Have each child sit in his rectangle with pencil and paper in hand; then tell students that they are each sitting on a raft that is lost at sea. Give each student a handful of cereal and a small cup of water to simulate the only food he has to survive. Then have the student write about how he feels being lost at sea. How did he become lost? What are his fears? How will he survive? For an added effect, play a tape of sea-related background music.

Paula Crew—Grs. 4–6
Rockway School
Springfield, OH

Help Is On The Way!

When one of my students hits a roadblock in choosing a character's name or setting for a story he's writing, he turns to his classmates for help. The troubled author simply writes a heading on the chalkboard (such as "kind neighbor, unmarried, female"). Then any student who has a suggestion writes it under the heading. After that the student has a number of ideas from which to choose—all without interrupting his classmates.

Christine Huiras—Gr. 6
Cedar Grove Elementary
Cedar Grove, WI

Colorful Characters

When it comes to motivating students to write at the end of the year, I call on a colorful cast of characters! First I instruct each student to create a one-of-a-kind character with a catchy name that uses alliteration (for example, Designer Dollie, Jenny Jewels, or Tornado Tim). Next I ask each child to write a humorous story about her character. After the stories are proofread and recopied, I direct each child to use items from home to create a costume that will transform her into her character. I take a photo of each child wearing her costume; then we compile these stories and pictures into a class book. During free time, a student can read through the book, choose a story she likes, and write another adventure about that character.

Betty Bowlin—Gr. 4, Henry Elementary, Ballwin, MO

Strange Visitor

Improve descriptive writing and character development with this fun activity. Secretly select one student to bring an unusual, mismatched outfit of clothing to school and put it on before writing class. Instruct him to enter the classroom, clap his hands to get everyone's attention, and walk out of the room. As a class, brainstorm a description of the student and record students' responses on the chalkboard. Invite the dressed-up child back into the room and check the class's description for accuracy. Follow up by having each student write a descriptive paragraph about himself so that someone would be able to use it to pick him out of a crowd. Collect and redistribute the papers; then have students guess whom each paragraph describes.

Betty Bowlin—Gr. 4, Henry Elementary, Ballwin, MO

Whales in the ocean,
Swimming around and around
In the sea so blue.

Poetry Inspired By Art

Link haiku and symmetry with this simple art activity. Give each student a 9" x 12" sheet of construction paper to place on her desk. Drop a splash or two of paint on each student's paper. Have the student fold her paper in half greeting card–style, press the two halves together, then unfold the paper. Next instruct the student to write a haiku about what she sees in the paint blotch. After the paint dries, staple each poem to its artwork and post the project in the room.

Susan A. Ferguson—Gr. 5
Byram Intermediate School
Stanhope, NJ

My Buddy

Your next bulletin board is just a writing assignment away! Have each student bring in his "buddy"—a special blanket, a teddy bear, or another object—from his early childhood days. Then have the student write a paragraph explaining what his buddy meant to him. Take a picture of each student with his buddy. Display the pictures and paragraphs on a bulletin board titled "Meet My Buddy!"

James Embrescia—Gr. 4
Hilltop Elementary
Beachwood, OH

Describe your favorite season of the year.

Compare a tree in winter to a tree in summer.

Tell about a time you experienced a severe storm.

A "Write" Idea!

End those frequent complaints of "I don't know what to write about!" with this easy idea. Have each student bring in a small assignment pad. Throughout the day—whenever a topic comes up that would be good to write about—call out, "A 'write' idea!" Then have the class brainstorm two or three related topics to write about. Have each student record the topics in her assignment pad. After only a few such sessions, your students' pads will be packed with writing ideas!

Terry Healy—Gifted K–6, Eugene Field Elementary, Manhattan, KS

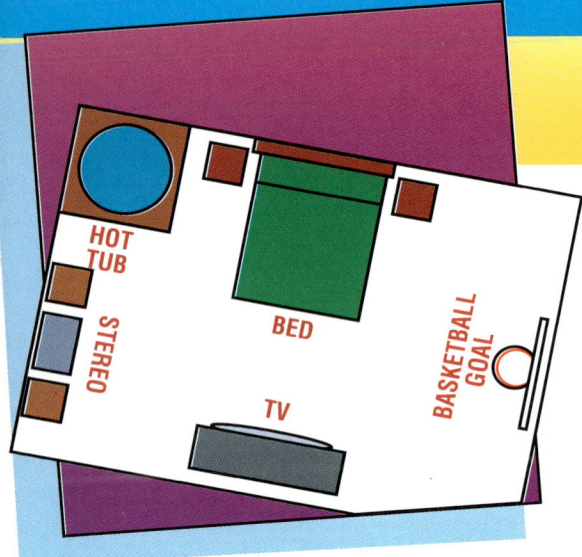

Dream Bedroom

To begin a descriptive writing activity, I first ask each of my students to imagine his dream bedroom. The idea usually catches on quickly as students brainstorm various ideas to include in their descriptions. Students edit each other's writings before making their final copies. To complete the project, each student draws a diagram of his dream bedroom on a sheet of 11" x 17" paper according to his written description. The diagrams and writings are displayed for everyone to enjoy.

Beth Price—Gr. 5, Logan Intermediate School, Bridgeport, NJ

Star Author

Reward a hardworking writer with this star treatment! Keep a supply of cut-out stars on hand in your classroom. When you find a student whose finished work is done particularly well, ask for permission to read it aloud to the class. After reading the selection, have each of your students write something positive about the work on a cut-out star. Display the featured writing along with the complimentary stars on a "Star Author" bulletin board. Students will love seeing their work displayed and receiving positive praise from their peers!

Jessica Nardi—Language Arts Resource
Hillsborough Elementary
Livingston, NJ

The Writing Rack

Need an easy and fun way to get your students organized for writing? Purchase a folding, wooden laundry rack and attach to it a colorful sign labeled "Our Writing Rack." Collect a class supply of clothespins; then write a student's name on each one. As each student completes a rough draft of a writing project, have her clip her paper to the rack. Explain to your class that good writers let their ideas and writing "dry" overnight. The next day have each student unclip her paper and create a final draft. The Writing Rack not only keeps everyone from losing her rough draft, but also is a handy tool for checking student progress at a glance.

Betsy Rumberger—Gr. 4, Harrisburg Academy, Wormleysburg, PA

Our Readers Write

Jurassic Prose

Reel in reluctant researchers by combining research with creative writing. Begin by reading fictional stories that contain accurate dinosaur information (for example, Oliver Butterworth's The Enormous Egg). Have students research several species of dinosaurs, noting when they lived, their habitats, their body structures, and their eating habits. Next have students weave their dynamic dinosaur facts into creative story lines to create fabulous factual fiction. Allow the introduction of human characters (who did not live during the dinosaur age) only if students provide a logical explanation. These "dino-mite" stories are sure to go down in history!

Pamela Sloan, Jackson County Middle School, Jefferson, GA

Time-Traveling Field Trip Visits The Dinosaurs!

Editing Student Writing

Marking up a nearly completed draft usually means that the student has to entirely rewrite his paper. Clear up this editing dilemma by clipping a clear overhead transparency to each draft. As the paper is edited, the writer, a peer, or the teacher marks on the transparency using a water-based pen. With this method, the student can revise his paper without having to totally rewrite a new draft. The transparency can be easily cleaned for reuse later.

Kathi Sweere—Gr. 5
Florence Mattison Elementary
Conway, AR

Journals Organizer

Try this tip to help you keep your student journals organized. Purchase an inexpensive dish rack at a department store or garage sale. Space journals evenly in the rack's plate dividers. If desired, write your students' names on tabs near the side of the rack so they'll always know which journal slots are theirs.

Maura Hendrickson—Grs. K–6, Hall County District #5
Wood River, NE

Journal Buddies

If you don't have time to respond to students' journals every day, try this idea. Assign each student a journal buddy. Each day have buddies exchange journals and write responses to their partners' entries. Periodically collect the journals to add your comments. This activity gives students immediate feedback and provides them with additional writing practice.

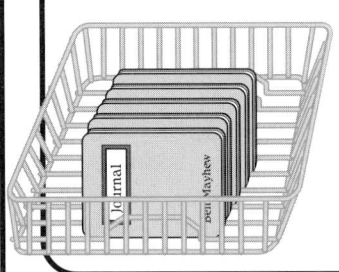

10-1
Last night my dog, Sasha, had to go to the vet. He's sick. Today we'll find out what's wrong.

Megan—I'm sorry to hear about Sasha. My dog was sick too last year. The vet really helped him.

Pam Doerr, Elizabethtown School District, Elizabethtown, PA

Welcome To Our School!

It's a stressful time when a child enters a new school at midyear. To ease the anxiety for new students, my fourth graders created "Welcome To Whiteley School" booklets. First we brainstormed and listed important information, plus our classroom and school routines. Each student chose an item from the list and created a booklet page to explain it. A personal introduction and photo was also included on each page to help a new classmate match faces with names. What a worthwhile writing project!

Barbara Benton—Gr. 4
Frank C. Whiteley School
Hoffman Estates, IL

Loves animals
Always on time
Responsible
Reads a lot
Young and energetic

Begin With Acrostics

At the beginning of the school year, take snapshots of students in groups of two or three. Cut the photos so that each student has a picture of herself. Give each student a 9" x 6" sheet of construction paper on which to paste her picture. Instruct the child to write the letters of her name in a column beside the picture; then have her use each letter to begin a word or phrase that tells something about herself. Post the finished acrostics on a bulletin board entitled "The World's Greatest Class!" Students will enjoy getting to know each other by reading their classmates' acrostics. Plus the board will make a great Open House display!

Joyceann Dreibelbis—Gr. 4, Kean Elementary, Wooster, OH

Write To Us!

Whenever a popular student moves away, remedy the feelings of loss with a letter-writing campaign! Bring in a class supply of letter-sized envelopes and stamps. Review the form for addressing envelopes with students; then direct each student to address an envelope to himself, stamp it, and place it in a large manila envelope. Have a group of students make a large poster that says "Write To Us!" Let each student write a short message on the poster. Fold the poster, put it inside the large envelope, and mail it to the student who moved. The next day have each student write a letter to the child who moved away. Mail these letters inside another large envelope. The student who moved will have the terrific treat of receiving two special packages—and your students will have the fun of waiting for a reply!

Julia Alarie—Gr. 6, Essex Middle School, Essex, VT

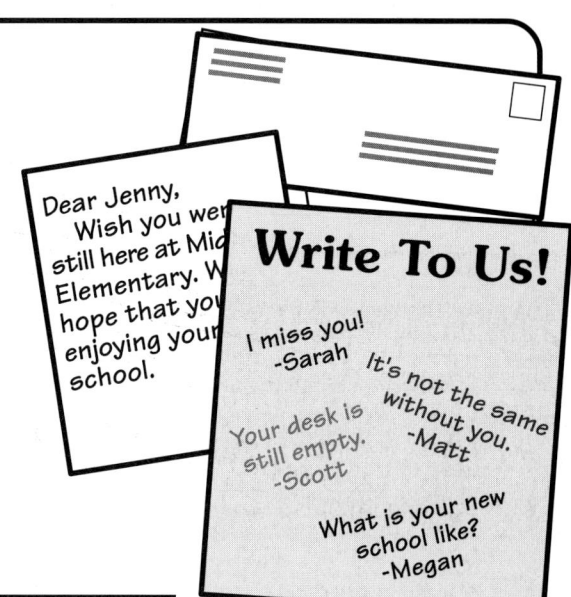

Journal Idea

Each Friday for their journal assignment, my students write to me and tell about the books they're currently reading. I write a brief response to each student in his journal, asking questions that encourage him to focus on character traits, setting, predictions, etc. My students are much more eager to read their books, knowing that they can write to me in their journals and I will respond.

Susan Barnett—Gr. 6
Northwest Elementary
Ft. Wayne, IN

"Spooktacular" Stories

Each October I hold a creative-writing and pumpkin-decorating contest for my fourth graders. In order to participate, the students have to enter "spooktacular" stories along with their decorated pumpkins. I have other teachers judge the stories and pumpkins. The judges select the most unusual, scariest, weirdest, most original, and cutest entries. The pumpkins and stories are displayed in the hall for the other students to enjoy.

Angela Pickich—Gr. 4
Oak Park Elementary
Ocean Springs, MS

Flashback

To help my students recall what they've learned from the previous week and to prepare them for the week ahead, I have them "flashback" every Monday morning. I put students in small groups and have them list by subject as much information as they can remember from their studies last week. The group that recalls the most earns a treat.

Deanna Wyrick—Gr. 4
Aboite Elementary
Fort Wayne, IN

Monstrous Poetry

Create a class full of musing monsters with this spooky poetry activity! Play a tape of scary special effects while you read a monster picture book aloud, such as *No Such Thing* by Jackie French Koller (Boyds Mills Press, Inc.; 1997) or *A Monster in My House* by Elisa Kleven (Dutton Books, 1998). Then give each student a 9" x 12" sheet of light-colored construction paper and an index card. Have each student tape the card in the middle of the paper. Then have her create an original monster around the card using crayons, markers, and other art supplies. Direct her to cut around the outline of her monster. Next have the student write a creepy monster poem on notebook paper. When her poem has been peer-edited and revised, have her rewrite it on the card before sharing her monster poem with the class.

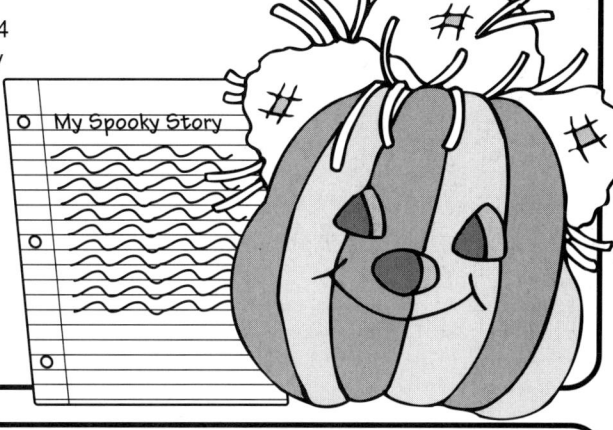

Judy Wetzel, Woodburn School, Oakton, VA

Super Sentence Contest

My class participates in a weekly Super Sentence Contest. Each student is provided with a large index card, which he uses weekly to record his super sentence. To begin, I give the class a simple, two- to three-word sentence. Each student then transforms it into one with lots of vivid adjectives, adverbs, and action verbs. I choose four or five of the best sentences, from which the class selects a final winner. I reward the winner with a small prize and post his card in the classroom.

The powdery white snow was incredibly cold.

Kelli Sanders—Gr. 4
Clayton Elementary, Clayton, NC

Check It Out

Check out this tip for a unique way to display students' writing or other work. Purchase an inexpensive plastic or paper checkered tablecloth to use as your bulletin-board background. Staple students' compositions to sheets of red and white construction paper; then mount the papers on the board. Use this same idea to create a display of important class reminders and school news!

Chana Rochel Zucker—Gr. 5
Be'er Hagolah School, Brooklyn, NY

Pen Pal Stationery

Create personalized class stationery by attaching your students' photographs around the perimeter of an 8 1/2" x 11" sheet of paper. Duplicate a class set of the sheet. Instruct each student to first write a descriptive paragraph about herself on a scrap piece of paper; then have her copy her edited paragraph—without identifying herself—onto the stationery. Challenge your pen pals to identify their letters' authors using the information in the paragraphs and the photos on the stationery. Be sure to send the teacher a key so that pen pals can check their sleuthing ability.

Cathy Woodward, McKinley Elementary, Newton, KS
Denise Johnson, Lundgren Elementary, Topeka, KS

Governors Quilt

As a special project to promote letter writing and social studies, my class made a governors quilt. Each child wrote to two governors. With each letter, students included a square piece of cloth for the governor to sign. Students asked the governors to sign the squares with permanent markers and return them as soon as possible. We got a great response! Along with most quilt squares that were returned, we received information and articles about the states and the governors themselves. After stitching the quilt together, we displayed it and all of the other items in our school. We plan to donate the quilt to a historical park or public library at the end of the year.

Cathy Ogg
Happy Valley Elementary
Johnson City, TN

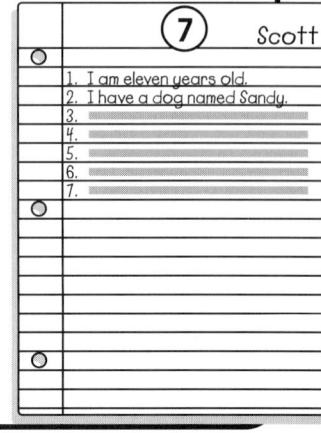

*James B. Hunt
Governor
North Carolina*

Comics And Current Events

Make the news a lead-in to learning with this hands-on activity! Collect a class supply of newspapers. Have each student choose a comic strip and a newspaper article. Direct her to trace her comic strip onto tracing paper, leaving the speech balloons blank. Then instruct her to carefully read her article and write dialogue about it in her strip's speech balloons. Have students color their strips before posting the work on a bulletin board. How's that for a newsworthy way to sharpen reading-comprehension, summarizing, and main-idea skills!

The United States and China signed a trade agreement today.

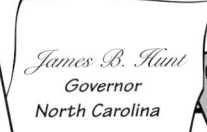

Leslie Reeves—Gr. 5
Santa Rita Elementary
Midland, TX

All About You

Ask each child to select a number between 1 and 15 and write it inside a circle at the top of his paper. Then have the student write facts—equal to the number written at the top of his paper—he'd like to share about himself. Since some students would be more comfortable communicating via a written format than they would be if speaking before a group, you're sure to gain valuable information about your less-outgoing kids. And you'll also reap insights into students' writing and vocabulary skills!

Jo Farrimond
Foster Middle School, Tulsa, OK

⑦ Scott
1. I am eleven years old.
2. I have a dog named Sandy.
3.
4.
5.
6.
7.

Friendly-Letter Friend

You can be sure that your class will remember how to organize a friendly letter with the following student-friendly diagram:

Deborah Johnson—
 Special Education
Loma Linda Elementary
Phoenix, AZ

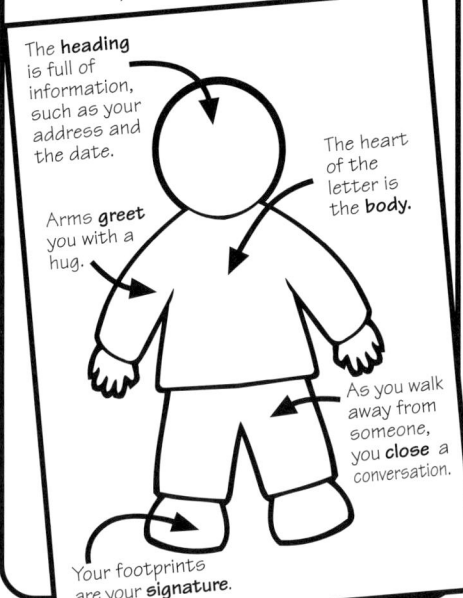

Simple Sentences

Tired of writing and rewriting sentences to be corrected on the chalkboard? Instead write incorrect sentences on sentence strips and laminate them. Have volunteers use overhead pens to place proofreading marks where changes are needed. Then have each student write the corrected sentences in her journal to discuss at a later time. Simply wipe off the marks, and the strips are ready to use again and again.

Cathy Ogg—Gr. 4, Elizabethton, TN

Writer's Block

Looking for a creative way to display your students' writing projects? Try this student-decorated bulletin board. I outline the layout of our town, Middletown, on a bulletin board. Then I have the class add representations of our local shops and businesses to the display. I title the bulletin board "Middletown Writer's Block" and display each student's writing around the illustrations.

Kathy Scavone—Grs. 4–5
Coyote Valley School
Middletown, CA

Weekly Journalist

Building a class scrapbook of a different sort is a snap with my simple idea! Each Monday I select one student to be the journalist of the week. This student uses a disposable camera to take a picture of anything he chooses. Once the film is developed, the student writes a description to go along with the picture that he took. I put all the pictures and descriptions into a scrapbook for free-time viewing.

Melanie Bruse—Gr. 5
Jordan Ridge Elementary
South Jordan, UT

Welcome To The World!

Looking for a fun way to review letter-writing skills? When a student announced she had a new baby sister, I asked each child in my class to write a friendly letter to little Julia. In the letters, the students were to welcome her into the world and share about their favorite books, hobbies, movies, etc. Not only did my students have a great learning experience, but they also created a one-of-a-kind keepsake for baby Julia.

Mary Lynn Vinal
Dodge Elementary
East Amherst, NY

Grand-Slam Publishing Party

To celebrate the writing successes of the past year, my class holds a publishing party centered on a baseball theme. The evening program is divided into nine "innings." Each inning features a small group of students who share a specific type of writing (haiku, descriptive paragraphs, etc.) with the parents in attendance. In the seventh inning—the "stretch"—we take a break and do some clever vocabulary-stretching activities. In the ninth inning, we close the program with a choral reading of the poem "Casey At The Bat." A snack of peanuts and popcorn ends this fun celebration of our winning season as writers.

Pat Madden—Gr. 4, Corpus Christi School, Lansdale, PA

Animal Quotations

I've found a really amusing and motivational way to teach my students how to write direct quotations. Using animal pictures from old calendars, I ask my students to write what they think that animal would say if it could talk. The results are often hilarious. The class votes to decide the funniest quote, but I only allow students to choose from quotations that are correctly written. It's amazing how interested my kids have become in punctuating their ideas correctly!

"Look, it's superman!" quipped Pierre the penguin.

Vivian Kannon—Gr. 4
Lakeview Annex
Nashville, TN

Writers' Blocks

Whenever my students are writing in Writing Workshop, they have an easy way of letting me know when conferences are needed. Instead of raising his hand and sitting idle, a student picks a toy alphabet block from the writing center and places it on his desk. This allows the child to continue working until I see the conference-needed signal. "Down time" for student writers is virtually eliminated!

Robin Kennedy—Gr. 5
Ashley River Creative Arts Elementary School
Charleston, SC

"OARP"

To add a twist to my students' literature circles, they now "OARP." When a group is given a reading assignment, each student writes an OARP response in his journal. OARP stands for the following:
  Opinion: how the student felt about the selection
  Action: what happened in the selection
  Reaction: how the characters react to the action
  Prediction: what the students think will happen next
My students love to OARP, and I love listening to their discussions!

Ellen Mucha—Grs. 5–8 Language Arts, Immaculate Heart of Mary–St. Luke's
Minneapolis, MN

Journal Log

Help late-arriving or absent students catch up on journal-writing assignments with this simple tip. Each day choose one student to copy the day's writing prompt in a special notebook and date it. Then you have a record of all journal prompts *and* the dates on which they were assigned. When Johnny arrives from a dental appointment, just send him the journal log!

Write about your favorite Thanksgiving meal.
(November 9, 2000)

Kathy Kayiran—Gr. 4
Westwood Basics Plus Elementary, Irvine, CA

Writing To Pen Pals

When writing to pen pals, I supply my students with plain, prestamped postcards from the post office. On one side they write or type their messages and address the cards. On the other side, they draw pictures of their town, school, families, etc. Our pen pals really enjoy receiving these personalized postcards.

Janet Moody—Gr. 4
Truman Elementary
Lafayette, LA

Vacation Journals

Since our school is located in a farming community, many families don't get to take extended vacations except during the school year. I don't like to burden my fifth graders with a lot of work while they're on vacation, so I provide each student with a blank journal. I ask that the student write in the journal about the family's daily activities, keep a mileage log, and record money that is spent. Students use practical skills and are always excited to share their journals when they return to school. They also have wonderful keepsakes of their trips!

Shannon Criss—Gr. 5, Grant Elementary, Ephrata, WA

Haiku Note Cards

For Mother's Day, Easter, or any other special day, my students write haiku. I have students fold white paper to make note cards. Each student rewrites his haiku on the front of the card, then decorates it. After each child has created about six cards, he bundles them together with ribbon; then he gives his set of cards as a gift to a special someone.

Dale Lindberg—Gr. 5, Stone Scholastic Academy, Chicago, IL

Like A Diamond In The Sky

In March I have my students write diamante poems. The natural configuration of these poems makes them perfect for copying onto construction-paper kites (see the illustration). After each child has copied his poem on a kite cutout, I mount the kites on a bulletin board titled "Like A Diamond In The Sky."

Colleen M. Roy—Gr. 4
Assawompset School
Lakeville, MA

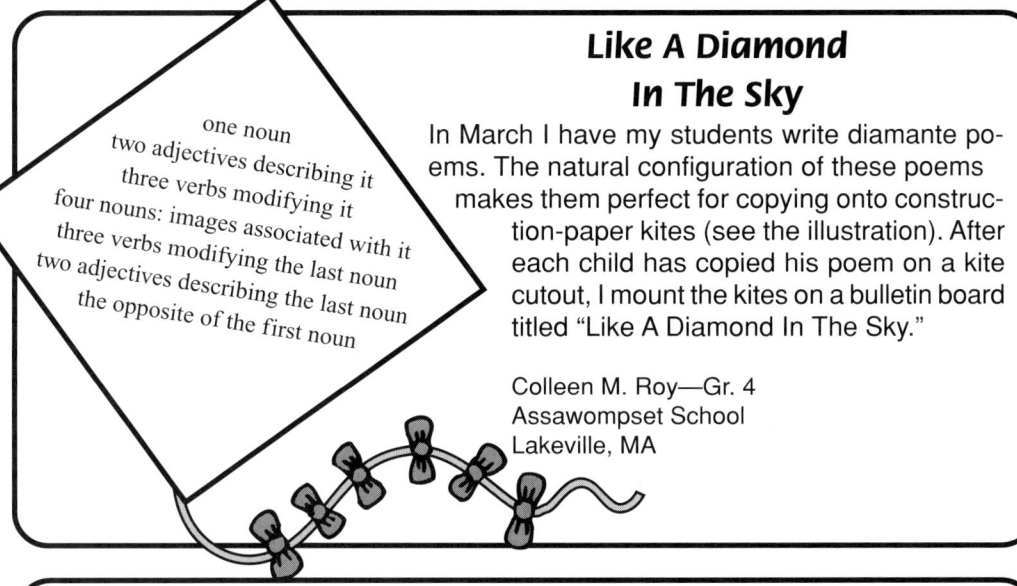

one noun
two adjectives describing it
three verbs modifying it
four nouns: images associated with it
three verbs modifying the last noun
two adjectives describing the last noun
the opposite of the first noun

"All About My Teacher" Class Book

Have students collectively make this end-of-the-year class book for a treasured keepsake. Supply each child with a sheet of paper. Have him write one or two paragraphs telling something about you and his favorite experiences in your class; then have him illustrate his page. Next have him write your name vertically on the back of his paper and use each letter to start a word or phrase that describes you. Bind all students' pages together between construction-paper covers and title the book "All About My Teacher." This special book will not only be a wonderful memento, but also a great icebreaker to share at next year's Open House.

Laura Sunley
Powell, OH

A Gift From The Heart

When my class decided to sponsor an elderly person for Christmas, we needed a way to finance the project. The solution was a collection of holiday recipes and students' original poems and illustrations. Students sold copies of the book for $1.00 each. What a great way to demonstrate the true spirit of Christmas and share our holiday work with families and friends!

Cindy Campbell—Gr. 4
Boswell Elementary
Lebanon, MO

Drop Me A Line!

Practice letter-writing skills all year long with this simple idea. At the beginning of the year, have each student bring stationery, a few stamps, and the addresses of several friends or family members to school. Store each child's supplies in a special folder. Each grading period, pull out the supplies and have each student write a letter to one of his chosen recipients. A great activity for Friday afternoon!

Candy Whelan, Garlough Elementary
West St. Paul, MN

Time To Read And Write

Develop fluent readers and writers with the help of your class calendar. Use the day's date to determine the amount of time students spend on sustained reading and writing. For example, on March 28 have students write for 28 minutes and then read silently for 28 minutes. Students will look forward to the time to read and write without interruptions.

Wendy Rodda—Grs. 5/6
Middleton, Nova Scotia, Canada

This Year I Learned...

Review the school year with this class book-making activity. Challenge each of several groups to list everything the class has learned this year. Next have a volunteer from each group come to the front of the room and write an item from his group's list on a sheet of chart paper. After everyone has added to the list, have each child select one item, write a brief reflection about it on a piece of paper, and illustrate his page. Bind these pages into a class book that you can use to pique the curiosity of next year's class!

Susan Keller—Gr. 5
Plumb Elementary
Clearwater, FL

Silly Synonym Stories

Give students practice using a thesaurus with the following nifty activity. Divide the class into groups. Provide each group with a familiar children's picture book and one thesaurus. Direct each group to work together to rewrite the book, replacing each noun and adjective with a synonym found in the thesaurus. Old stories such as *The Three Little Pigs* and *Cinderella* become quite fresh after being rewritten by students!

Martha Ennis, Blackmon Road Middle School
Columbus, GA

Character Poems

If you read to your class each day, here's how that routine can help you teach poetry writing! One day each month after reading to the class, introduce students to a specific type of poetry. Then have each child write and illustrate a poem of that type based on a character from your current novel. It's an easy way to teach poetry, check comprehension, and practice writing skills all at the same time!

Marlys Cole—Gr. 4
Roy Gomm School, Reno, NV

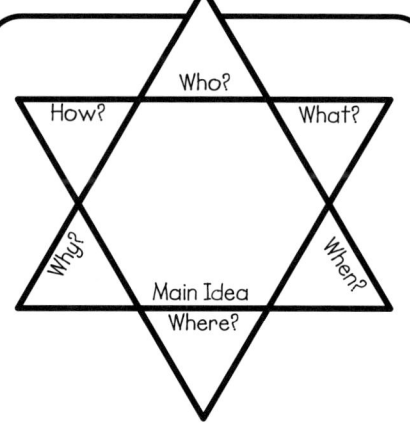

Reach For The Stars

Keep up with current events using this star-studded activity! Have each student bring in a newspaper article detailing a recent news event. Provide each student with a copy of the star pattern shown. Direct the student to complete each section of the star using information from her news article. Then have the student summarize the news-making event in a paragraph with the help of her star organizer. Display the completed stars and paragraphs on a bulletin board titled "Star-Studded Current Events."

Jane Cooney—Gr. 5
Guion Creek Elementary
Indianapolis, IN

Blooming Poetry

Brighten your room with a display that's abloom with student poetry! Have each student cut out a flower shape from loose-leaf paper and write a short poem about spring on it. Then have him color the flower with pastel colored pencils. Mount the poems on a bulletin board decorated with colorful construction-paper flowers. Add cut-out clouds and a sun for a cheerful finishing touch.

Jeannette Freeman—Resource
The First Lady Educational Program
San Juan, Puerto Rico

Mrs. kane's third-grade class is going to the cincinnati zoo today.

What's In The News?

Help your students keep up with current events while they practice proofreading sentences! Have students tell you facts about what is going on in world, state, community, school, or personal news. Include grammatical and punctuation errors as you record each sentence on a sheet of chart paper. Then have student volunteers use proofreading marks to correct your mistakes.

Michelle Pirog—Gr. 6 Resource, Raritan-Flemington Middle School, Flemington, NJ

Bulletin Boards

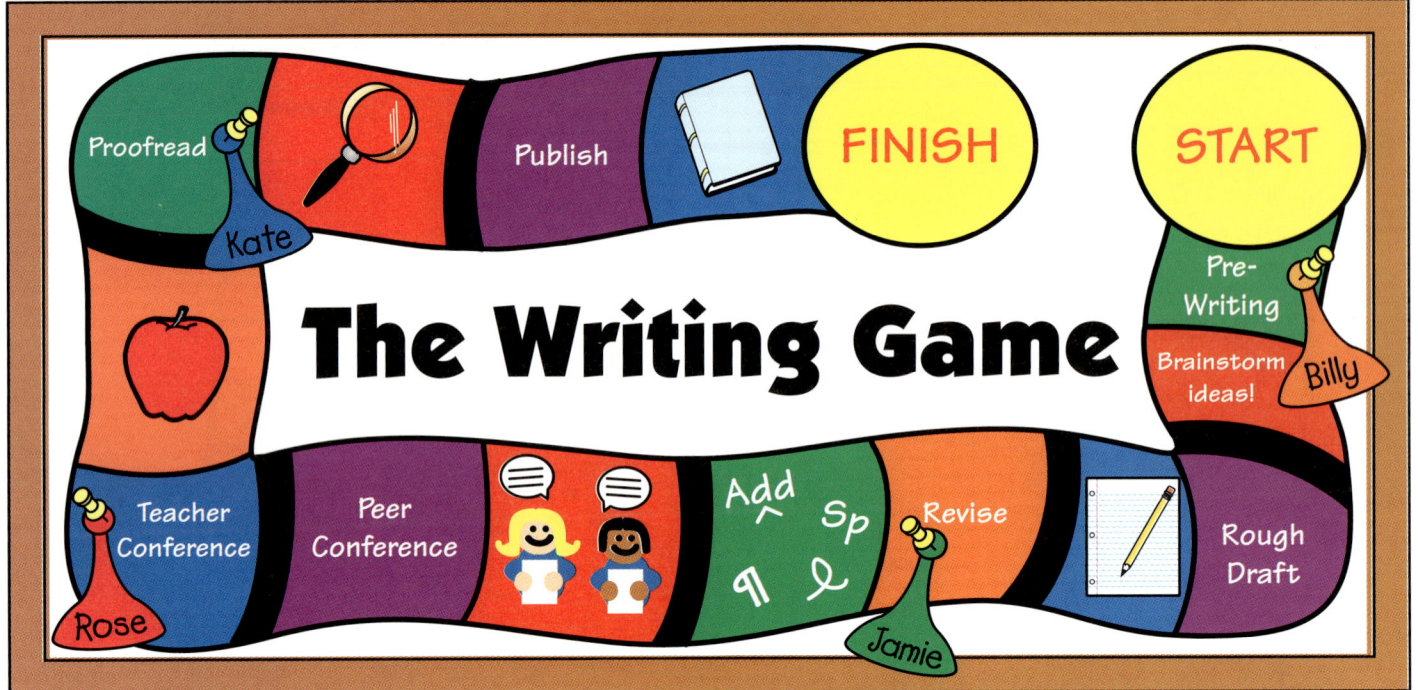

Keep track of students' progress on writing projects with this fun display! Draw and label a simple gameboard on a paper-covered board as shown. Also duplicate, cut out, and label a game pawn (like the one shown) for each student. As a child works on a writing piece, have her pin her pawn to the display to show where she is in the writing process. Point out to students that, just like in a board game, a writer may have to move her pawn back a few spaces as she works.

Kimberly Feldman—Gr. 6, Salt Brook Elementary, New Providence, NJ

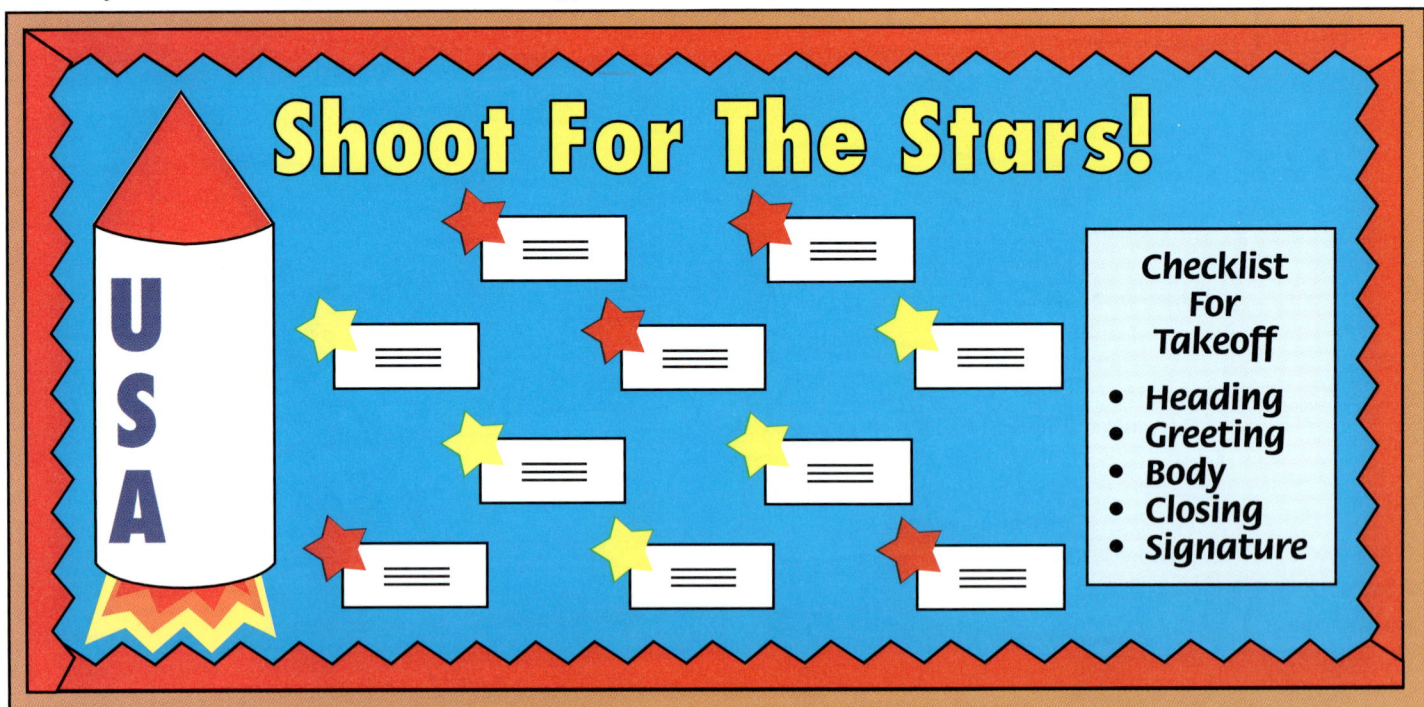

Help starstruck students sharpen their letter-writing skills with an out-of-this-world display! Ask your media specialist for reference books that list the addresses of popular entertainers, sports teams, and other famous folks. Select several addresses; then write each one on an envelope to post on a board that is decorated as shown. Encourage each student to choose an address and write a letter. If desired, provide stamped envelopes in which students can mail their letters.

Colleen Dabney—Grs. 6–7, Williamsburg Christian Academy, Williamsburg, VA

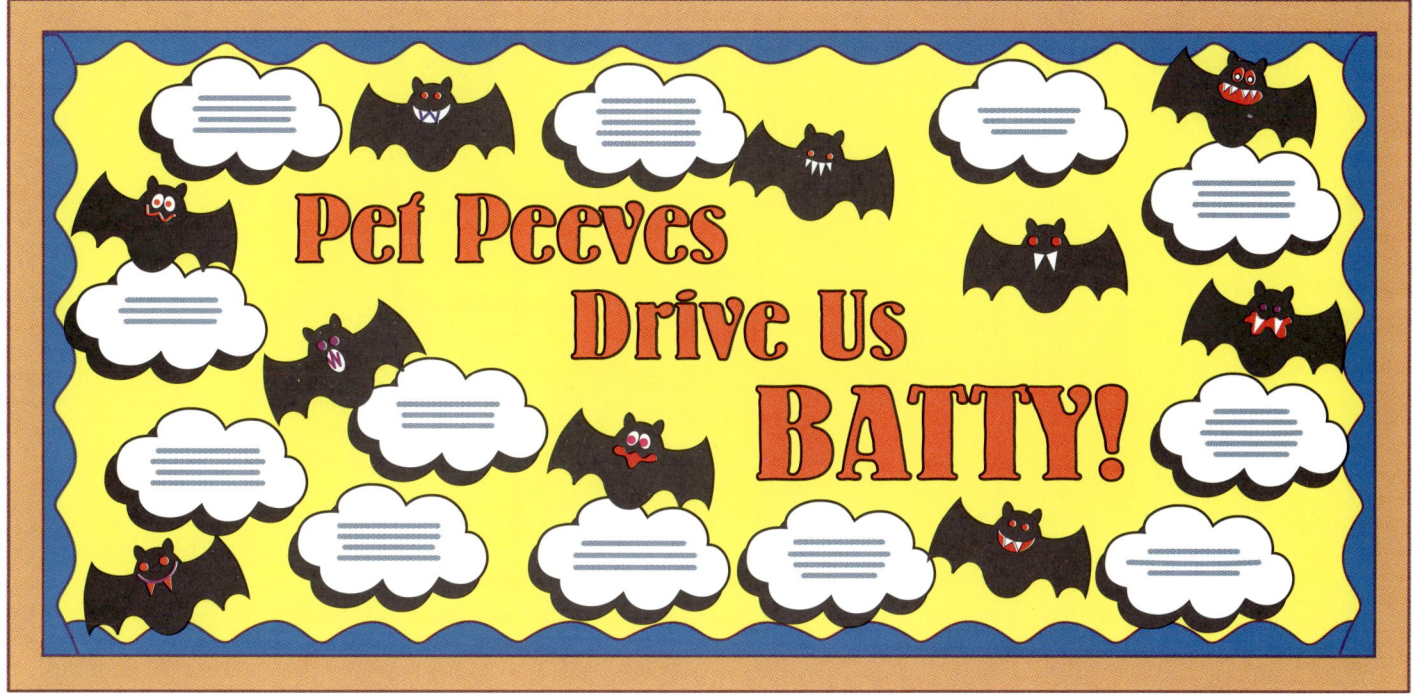

What pet peeve drives you batty? Have students interview family members and friends to find out their pet peeves. Give each student a bat pattern (like the one shown) to trace on black paper. Then have him cut out the bat and embellish it with paper eyes and fangs. Instruct the student to cut out one white and one black cloud from paper; then have him describe a pet peeve on the white cloud. Arrange the bat and cloud shapes on a board as shown.

Julia Alarie—Gr. 6, Essex Middle School, Essex, VT

Provide students with some sweet inspiration for creative writing with this hands-on display. Ask several students to draw and cut out pictures of their heads, wearing dreamy expressions. Mount these cutouts along the bottom of the board. Have another group of students draw and cut out a collection of sweet-tasting goodies, such as cookies, pies, cupcakes, etc. On the back of each goodie, write directions for a fun-filled activity, such as:
- List ten foods you think would be improved by adding chocolate chips.
- Name ten foods that each contain the name of a place—like Boston cream pie.
- Make five rebus puzzles that contain the "pie" sound, such as *python* and *pirate*.
- Write a description of cotton candy for someone who has never seen it before.

Attach these "sugarplums" above the sleeping heads with pushpins. Invite each student to visit the board during free time, remove a sweet, and complete its activity.

Karoleigh K. Nitchman—Grs. 4–6
Hurtsboro School Foundation
Hurtsboro, AL

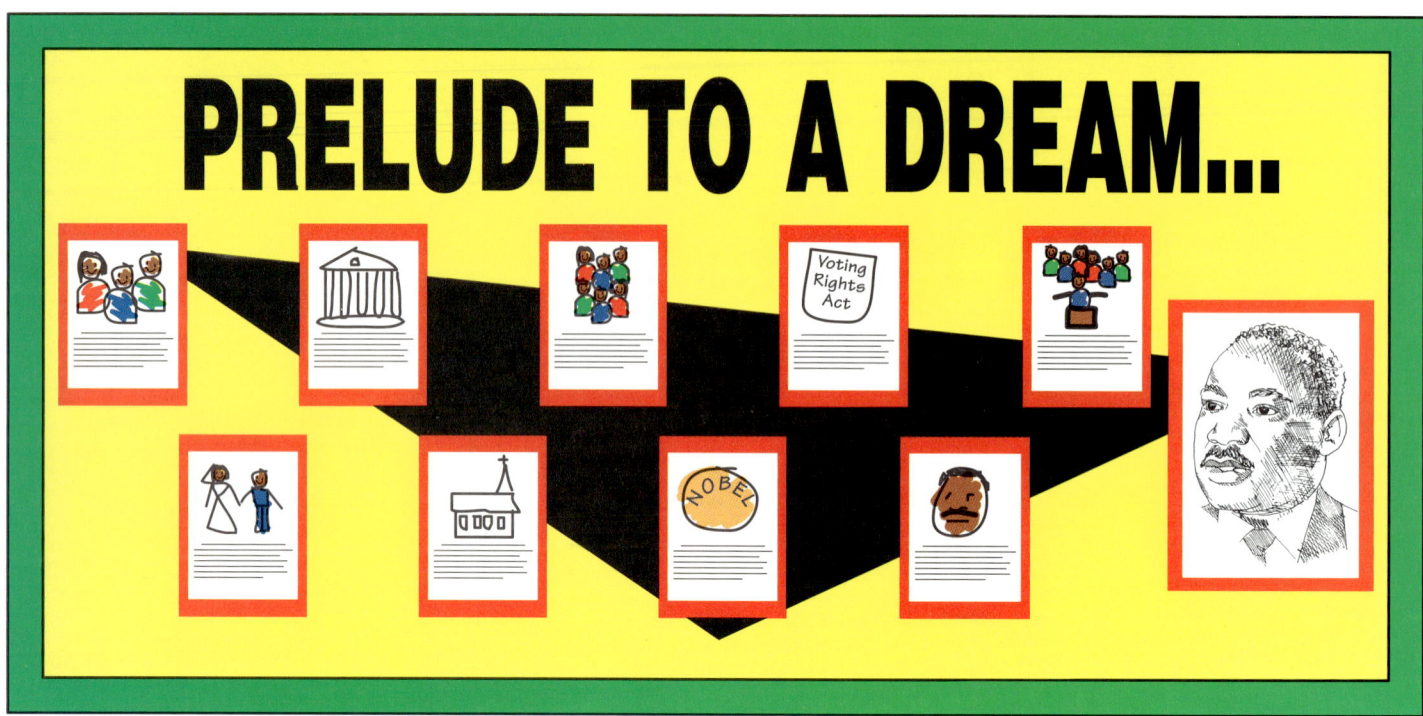

Celebrate the birthday of Dr. Martin Luther King, Jr., with this dramatic bulletin board. Instruct your students to work in pairs to research facts about King's life. Have each pair summarize its research in a paragraph and add an illustration. Mount these projects on red construction paper; then arrange them on the board on top of a large black triangle. Post a portrait of King at the wide end of the triangle as shown.

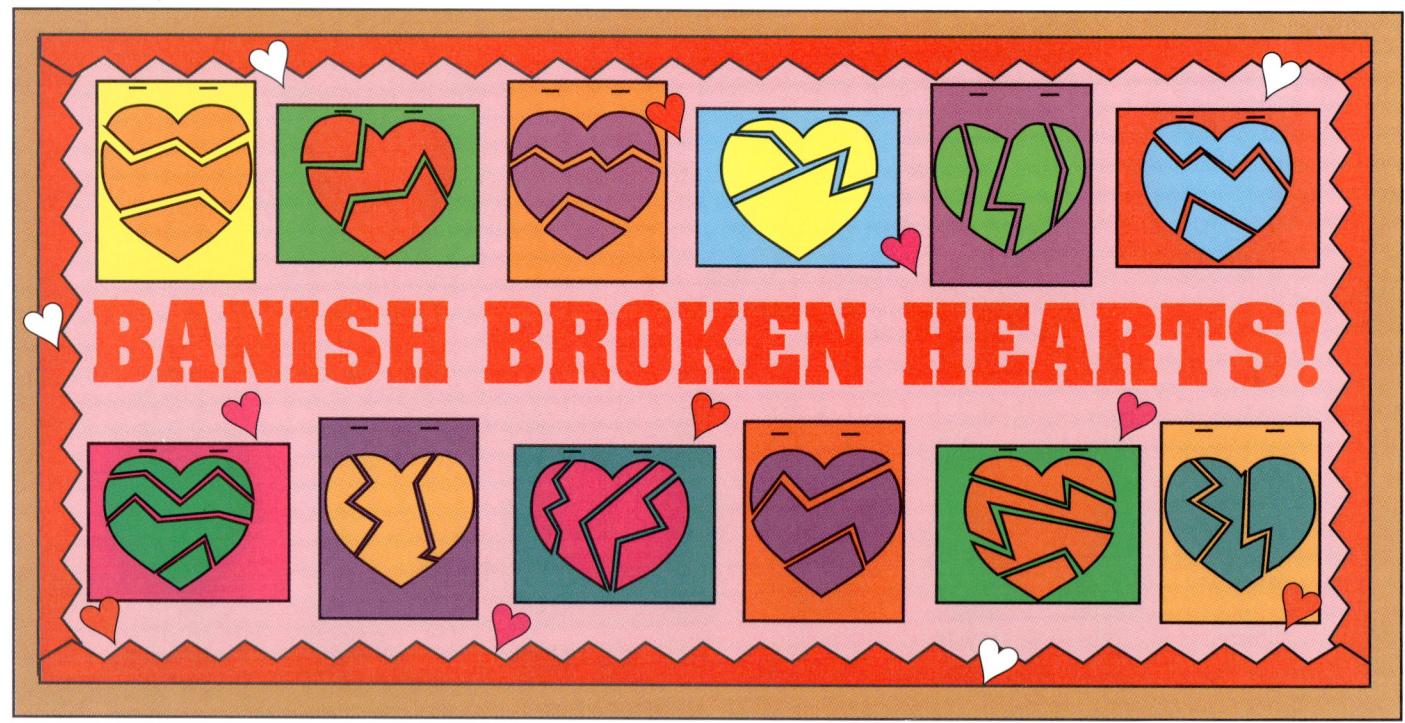

Have each student lightly draw two or more horizontal, diagonal, or vertical zigzag lines on a cut-out heart. After cutting along the lines, the student glues the pieces as shown on a contrasting color of paper. As a class, brainstorm conflicts that often arise between friends, family members, classmates, etc. Have each student write a solution to one of the problems on another sheet of paper. Place each child's heart project atop his solution; then staple the two papers at the top and mount them on the board.

Jackie M. Matthys—Gr. 4, Jackson-Keller Elementary, San Antonio, TX

For a bright Valentine's Day display, have each student create her own heart-shaped tartan. Explain to students that a tartan is a plaid pattern consisting of stripes of various widths and colors. The stripes cross at right angles against a solid background. Have each student fill a sheet of white construction paper with her tartan, using colored pencils, crayons, or markers; then have her cut a heart shape from the paper. Ask each student to write a paragraph about someone she is mad about. Post the paragraphs among the hearts.

Lisa Borgo—Gr. 4, East Hanover, NJ

For a St. Pat's display, duplicate a shamrock on green paper for each student. Have each student write about a time when she was lucky—without revealing her identity—on her shamrock. Then have her write her name lightly in pencil on the back of the cutout. Number the cutouts; then pin them to the board. Challenge students to guess the identity of each lucky person. Increase the mystery by adding shamrocks completed by staff members too!

Caroline Chapman, Vineland, NJ

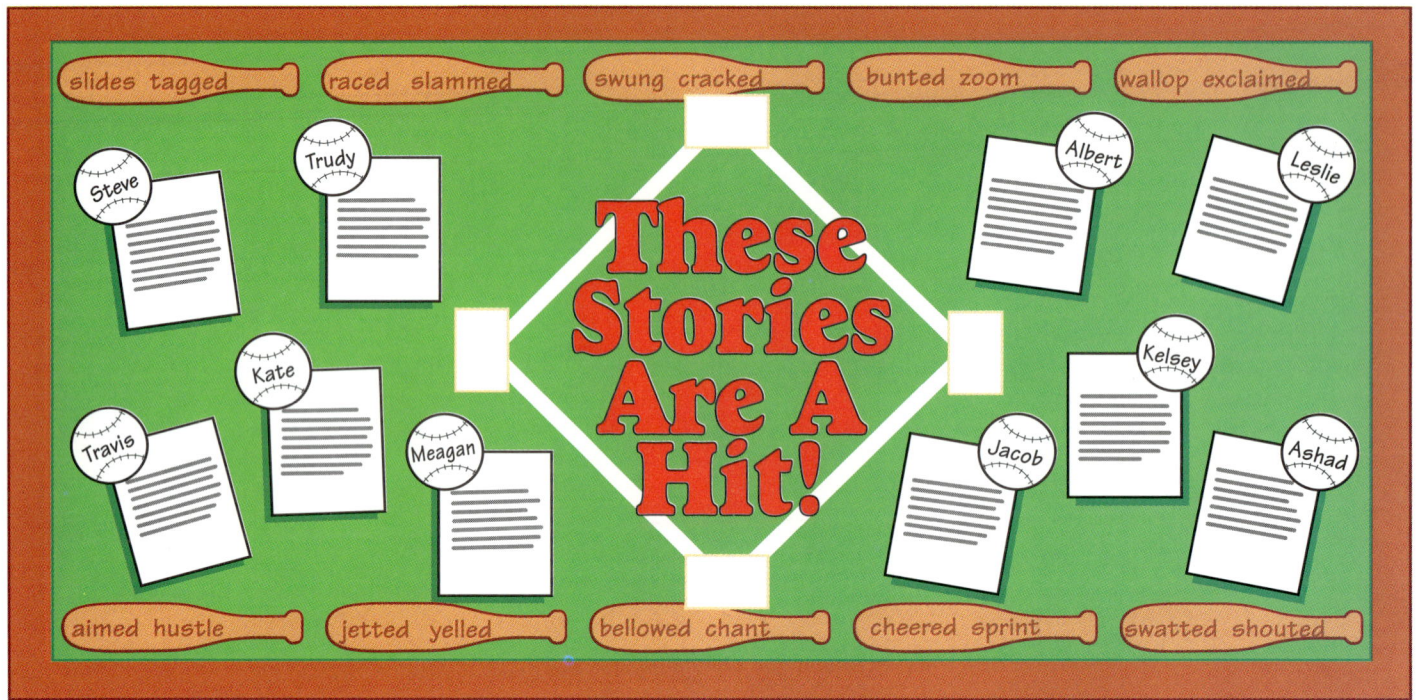

Celebrate America's love of baseball with this student-made display. Use masking tape to outline a baseball diamond on background paper. Add index cards for bases. Next provide each student with a baseball and bat cutout like the examples shown. Then brainstorm with students a list of action verbs associated with baseball. Have each child write a baseball story that includes lots of vivid verbs (each underlined); then have her list some of her action verbs on the cutout bat. Use the bats as a border for the board. Have each student write her name on the cutout baseball to post with her story.

Nancy Rafay, Bartlett, TX

Ladybug, ladybug, fly this way! Use these bright ladybugs to show off students' springtime poetry. To make a bug, have each student follow these steps:

1. Cut a seven-inch circle (body), a three-inch circle (head), and four two-inch circles (spots) from black construction paper.
2. Cut a seven-and-one-half-inch circle from red construction paper. Fold the circle in half and cut along the fold line to make two semicircles (wings).
3. Glue the head to the top of the body. Glue two spots on each wing.
4. Attach the wings to the top of the body with a brad.
5. Bend a black pipe cleaner (antennae) in half and attach it to the back of the head.
6. Glue your poem to the ladybug's body; then spread her wings so that your poem can be read and enjoyed by all.

Cindy Campbell—Gr. 4
Stoutland Elementary School
Stoutland, MO

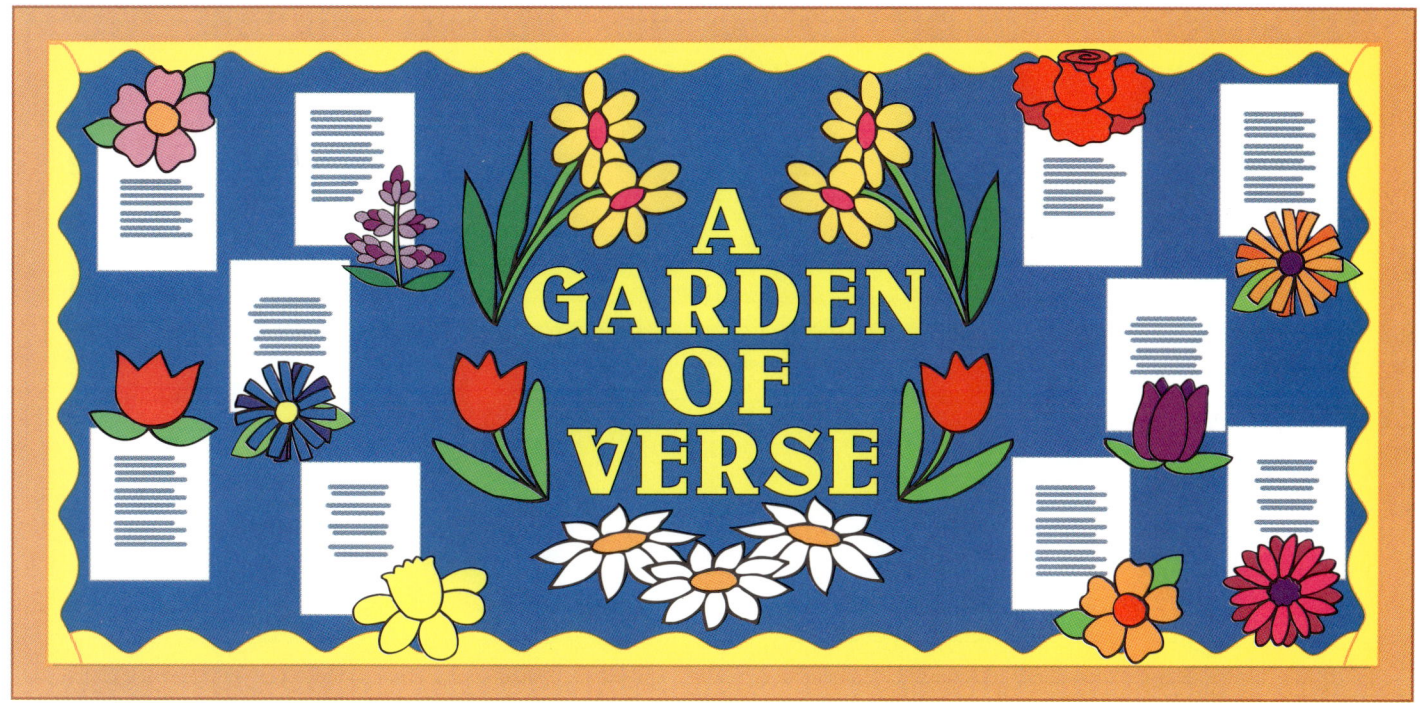

Cultivate a love of poetry with this easy-to-make display. Have each student cut out a large flower from a discontinued wallpaper book. Post each child's flower with a sample of her original poetry. Mount additional flowers around the title to complete your garden of glorious verses!

Colleen Dabney—Gr. 6, Williamsburg Christian Academy, Williamsburg, VA

Let the fun shine with this sunshiny how-to paragraph display! Purchase a class supply of bright yellow picnic plates (or spray-paint white paper ones). Have each child trace around her hands several times on yellow paper; then have her cut out the tracings and glue them around the rim of a plate to create a sun. Finally have her write a paragraph about how to have fun in the springtime sun and glue it in the center of the plate. Better grab those sunglasses!

Heidi Graves—Gr. 4
Wateree Elementary
Lugoff, SC

Highlight essays of the school year's most memorable moments with this eye-catching board. Pin a pair of child's overalls to the board. Then provide each student with an apple pattern like the one shown. Have each student cut out the apple pattern and tape a photo of himself on the cutout. Position each child's apple at the corner of his essay.

Tammy D. Taylor—Gr. 6, Franklin Elementary, Mt. Airy, NC

"Orange" you glad this end-of-the-year display is so simple to make? On an orange circle, have each student write a paragraph telling why one particular event, project, or activity made the year so much fun. Then display the circles with an enlarged orange cutout as shown. Or combine students' paragraphs—each written on a purple grape cutout—into a bunch on a board titled "Fifth Grade Was A Bunch Of Fun!"

Theresa Hickey—Gr. 4, St. Ignatius School, Mobile, AL

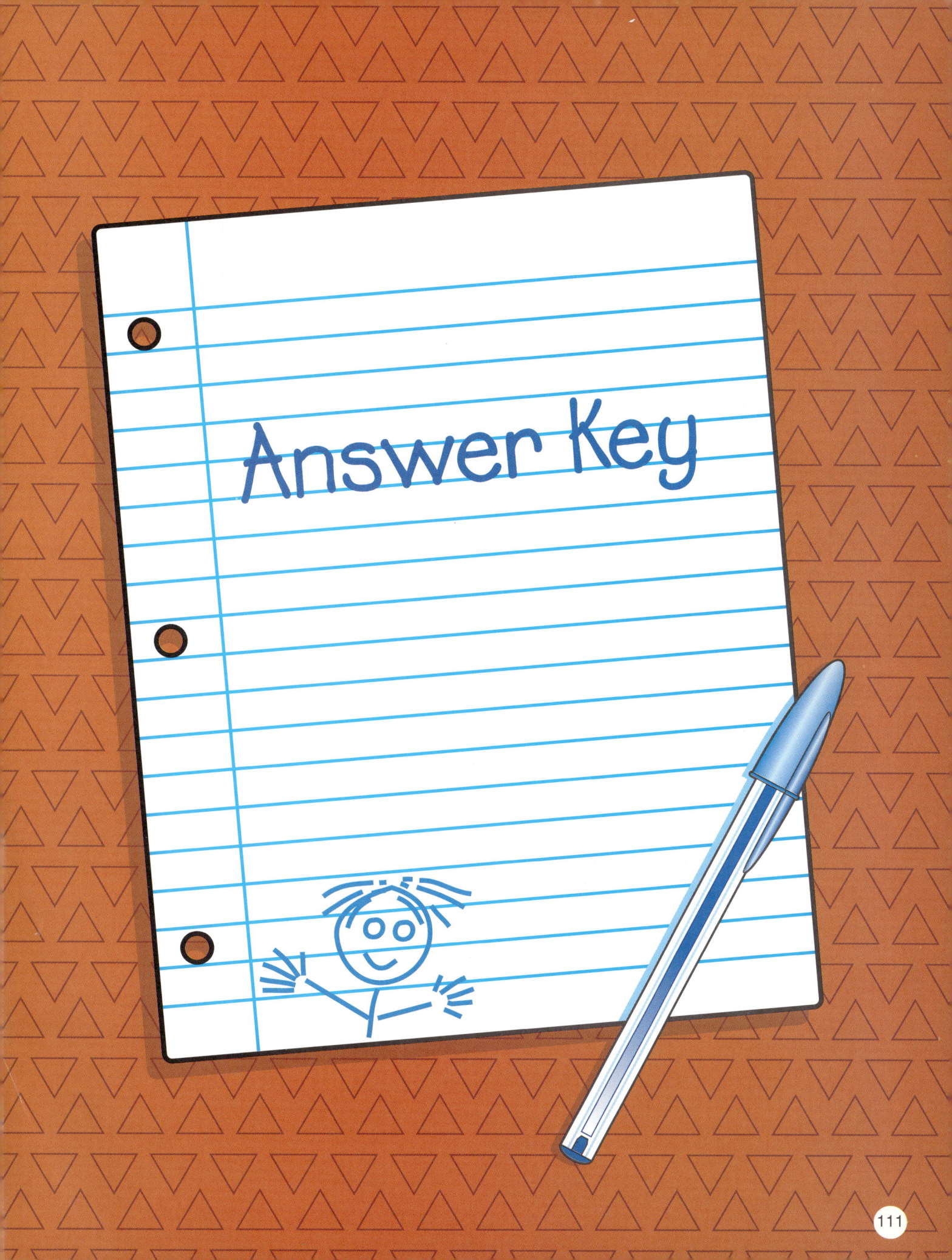

Answer Key

Page 36
Answers may vary slightly.
1. give reasons why homework is important
2. give reasons why homework should not be assigned on weekends
3. tell different ways that kids could earn money
4. tell various ways that money is different around the world
5. describe the unforgettable family vacation
6. tell how family vacations can be hazardous to your health
7. explain how hobbies of today are different from hobbies enjoyed by parents
8. give reasons why stamp collecting is a fascinating hobby

Answer to Bonus Box: The topic sentence is "Shopping malls are fun." Details would give reasons why shopping malls are fun.